THE GREAT THEMES OF SCRIPTURE:
OLD TESTAMENT

The Great Themes of Scripture

OLD TESTAMENT

Richard Rohr
and Joseph Martos

Nihil Obstat: Rev. Hilarion Kistner, O.F.M.
Rev. John J. Jennings

Imprimi Potest: Rev. Jeremy Harrington, O.F.M.
Provincial

Imprimatur: +James H. Garland, V.G.
Archdiocese of Cincinnati
March 31, 1987

The *nihil obstat* and *imprimatur* are a declaration that a book or pamphlet is considered to be free from doctrinal or moral error. It is not implied that those who have granted the *nihil obstat* and *imprimatur* agree with the contents, opinions or statements expressed.

All scriptural quotations that are not the free translations of the authors are taken from *The Jerusalem Bible,* published and copyright ©1966, 1967 and 1968 by Darton, Longman & Todd Ltd. and Doubleday & Company, Inc. Reprinted by permission of the publishers.

Book and cover design by Julie Lonneman

SBN 0-86716-085-3

Foreword

When I first gave the "Great Themes of Scripture" talks as a young priest in 1973, I little imagined how they would change my life, and apparently the lives of many others!

They changed mine because they were put on audiocassette—when not many Catholics were doing that yet (hard to believe!)—and therefore spread my message far beyond my original audience. But they changed my life in another way: Having my remarks made so public, I was sometimes forced to *believe* what I had now *said* about faith and the Word of God.

These talks led me on my own journey of faith—around much of the world—talking till I tired of my own voice, meeting countless Christians and communities, seeing sights and knowing sorrows that have further changed me, and now leading me to leave my beloved New Jerusalem in Cincinnati for a new venture in New Mexico.

I would rather have been like Terah, the father of Abraham, and stopped at more familiar Haran (Genesis 11:31), but I had unfortunately *talked* about the complete journey to Canaan. I would much rather have been like Aaron, the priest who himself formed the golden calf (Exodus 32:4), but I had unawares spoken of Moses, who railed at idolatry and was tortured with dissatisfaction. I could easier have been "a nice priest" (like my mother wanted), but now I had heard of Isaiah, Jeremiah, Amos and John the Baptist—from my own mouth on audiocassette! I could have quite easily been a "good" Christian, a pious charismatic, a dedicated minister of the system, but I had unthinkingly talked about—and talked to—this Jesus Man. I am trapped, even if not yet converted. My words returned again and again to condemn and console me.

There are two people that I must particularly "blame" for these tapes-now-become-book: First, Sister Pat Brockman, O.S.U., who talked me into taping them against my better judgment and my Franciscan humility. She was convinced that others might like to hear them and, with her loving optimism, convinced the wary staff at St. Anthony Messenger of the same. Further, her energetic realism said that we needed to make money for the new youth ministry that we were then involved in (which was eventually to become the New Jerusalem Community). Second, I must blame Father Jeremy Harrington, O.F.M., then editor of *St. Anthony Messenger* and now our most appreciated Provincial. He has the grace to affirm and believe in just about any friar! And so he did, and still does, with me and many others. Ah, the peril of loving friends!

There is also someone I must now thank—for taking my style of expression, that somehow seems to work as a speaking style, and making it into a readable prose style: I congratulate Joe Martos. He did what I was convinced was impossible. By the metamorphosis of love, patience (oh, so much!), and skill, he took my-spoken-words-trying-to-be-God's-Word and made them into a much better written word—which is still God's and mine, but also Joe's. And that is exactly what Scripture should be! Umm, the loves of perilous friends!

To be honest, I would probably say a lot of this differently now. Then I was young, convicted, surrounded by hope and easy joy. These are the necessary beginning words of the evangelist. I am happy I said them. Now I am older, chastened by failures, rejections, human suffering, study and the sophistications and nuances of supposed experience.

Do I now know more or less? Were these words adequate, or am I saying it better now? Which naivete is preferred, first or second? I am really not sure, and needn't be. I am just very grateful that I am "trapped" in these effusions of youthful Good News by the miracle of technology that Jesus and Paul never had. I wish they had, but for now I will content myself with wishing that Jesus and Paul, and all the holy crowd, will be able to speak to you through these sounds on paper, this desire to communicate on the part of God, Richard and Joe.

I think God Himself/Herself would agree that James Carroll's evaluation of his own words apply aptly to this book as well: "Most of it is heresy, some of it is absurd, and all of it is true."

Richard Rohr, O.F.M.
March 20, 1987
Center for Action and Contemplation
Albuquerque, New Mexico

Preface

This book is a work of collaboration. Like a Gilbert and Sullivan operetta or a Rodgers and Hammerstein musical, it is the combined effort of two persons. Each has his own special gifts, his own unique talents.

Richard's special gift is inspired and inspiring speaking. He has been recognized for this by being invited to preach and teach around the world, and by making a number of cassette recordings which have sold thousands of copies.

My own unique talent is clear and organized writing. People tell me that my first book really helped them understand the history of the Catholic sacraments even though they were not theologians. In my second book I was able to pull together information from psychology, sociology, history, theology and spirituality in order to present a contemporary evaluation of the sacraments in the life of the Church.

Readers who have listened to Richard Rohr's cassette series *The Great Themes of Scripture* will know where the inspiration for this book comes from. When I first undertook the task of editing those tapes to put them into print, I was hoping to smooth out the grammar here and there, introduce paragraphing to the continuous flow of Richard's ideas, and make as few alterations as possible. As my work progressed, however, it became clear that Richard's charismatic delivery could not be easily transcribed onto the printed page. I knew that I would have to add my own creative talent as a writer to his gift for spontaneous speaking if his ideas were to reach the wider audience who would benefit from having those cassettes in book form.

It has been a rewarding collaboration. Not only has Richard been an inspiration to me and a patient supporter of this project, but other members of the New Jerusalem Community in Cincinnati have also given of their time and talent in the earlier stages of this work. I would especially like to thank Walt Bassett for his practical advice and technical assistance and Sister Pat Brockman for the work she did on an earlier typescript of *The Great Themes*.

If our collaborative effort has been successful, this book will appear to be all of a piece with each chapter part of a unified whole. Readers may wonder which of us contributed what to the finished work. And if I would acknowledge that the words are often mine, I must always admit that the music is Richard's.

Joseph Martos
Allentown, Pennsylvania

Contents

Introduction

You are about to set out on a great adventure. The promise is upon you: Today the Lord will give you something new. All you have to do is hunger, and the Lord will give you what you desire. You have to come before the Lord expecting and wanting something more than you already have.

We get what we expect from God. When we have new ears to hear with, the Lord can speak a new word to us. When we no longer expect anything new or anything more from God, we are like nonbelievers, atheists for all practical purposes.

In this moment the Lord wants to speak something new to you. Not to believe in that, not to hope in that, is to have lost faith in the power of the Word of God.

The apostle Paul wrote to the Christian community in Rome, "I am not ashamed of the good news: it is the power of God saving all who have faith" (Romans 1:16). This is the power that I am talking about. I am not ashamed of this good news because I have seen the power, the life, the adventure, the vitality and the freedom that it has brought to many.

Never in my wildest imagination would I have chosen or planned when I was ordained to be doing what I am doing now.* I am a Franciscan, and when I was ordained my superiors asked me what I wanted to do as a priest. I said, first of all, that I

---

* The talks on which the chapters in this book are based were given in 1973.

1

wanted to preach, to have a chance in missions and retreats to communicate the power and the life of the Word of God to people. I said, secondly, that I would like to teach Scripture, which is what I had gotten my degree in. Thirdly, I said that I would be happy to return to the Indians in New Mexico where I had worked as a deacon.

Then they asked me what I would not like to do, and I said I would not like to work with teenagers. No offense to teenagers, but I felt a great need to get the Word to adults. Also, I was afraid that if I started working with teenagers, I would be too concerned about entertaining them and pleasing them and perhaps even watering down the gospel. But the Lord had different plans, and that first year of my priesthood I was asked to teach religion at a Franciscan high school for boys in Cincinnati.

That year I came to see that even sophomore boys were ready for something more, for something deeper. They were ready to be challenged. They were ready to hear the good news.

Soon after that I was asked to take charge of the youth retreats in the diocese. And out of that, in a few months time, in what can only be called a series of big and little miracles, a community began to be formed. I am now [1973] the leader of that community which we have come to call New Jerusalem, a community where four to five hundred of us meet for prayer and worship on Friday nights, a community that has been formed in prayer by the Word of God.

We have discovered that only the Word of God can truly form a community. Only the Word of God can truly teach us how to pray and how to believe. This is something new for many Catholics. We do not, for the most part, have a biblical spirituality. Many of us were trained on the Baltimore Catechism, and we lost the vision of people struggling with the mystery of God and walking the journey of faith. Only the Scriptures can communicate that vision to us.

The six chapters in this book make up volume one of a two-volume overview of the great themes of Scripture. As you go through them you will find that if you can get a feeling for these few great themes, somehow the whole Bible starts tying together. We begin to see the whole book from Genesis to

Revelation as communicating a single basic call for our lives. And to those who enter this dialogue with the Scriptures, one basic message is communicated, and that message is the good news. It is the same as what we have been calling the Word of God.

Jesus, of course, personifies that Word and sums it up. This is what the Word says: Know that you are saved, you are loved, you are unique, you are free. And know that you are on the way, you are going somewhere, your life does have meaning.

In many and varied ways, you will hear that good news in the following chapters. And you may never say, after hearing this Word, that you have not been evangelized. You have heard the good news, and nothing can ever be the same afterward.

The responsibility is yours. The Word is upon you. And you have the power to be set free in that Word.

CHAPTER ONE

The Call:
Introduction to the Word

The key to understanding the Scriptures is learning to recognize the great themes which appear again and again, in book after book, from the Old Testament to the New. Meditating on the passages in which those themes appear is one of the principal ways of opening our heart and mind to the Word which speaks to us through the Scriptures, for it is the same Word which the inspired authors listened to when they composed the sacred texts. Before mentioning those themes and discussing how they are developed in the Scriptures, however, it is important to say something about the Bible as the Word of God, and to introduce the books which make it up.

The Meaning of the Bible—Then and Now

The Bible is a record of people's experience of God's self-revelation. It is based on experience. The book did not fall from heaven. It was written by people listening to God. In the stories of the Hebrew people we see Yahweh, the God of Israel, gradually showing himself to be the hope and the promise of those who search for more. Their history became the wonderful work of God leading them forward into an ever greater unity and maturity as a community of faith.

The same is true for us. God saves us as a people. In the very process of bringing us together, he brings us to himself. And bringing us to himself, he brings us together.

Israel's faith in the power of God's Word is well expressed by the prophet Isaiah:

> A voice says, "Shout!" I answer, "What shall I shout?" It says, "All flesh is grass. Its beauty is like the wildflower's....The grass will wither, the flower will fade, but the word of our God will endure forever." (Isaiah 40:6-9)

The Israelites knew the power and the reality of the Word of God. A little later, the prophet says again:

> Yes, as the rain and the snow come down from the heavens and do not return without watering the earth, making it yield and giving growth to provide seed for the sower and bread for the eating, so the word that goes from my mouth does not return to me empty, without carrying out my will and succeeding in what it was sent to do. (Isaiah 55:10-11 JB)

This is what happened to Israel. You have to expect this to happen to you as well. It is a promise. The Word of the Lord does not lie. The Word of the Lord, when it is planted in fertile soil, has to yield 30-, 60- and 100-fold. In accepting this initiative of love from God, the Hebrew people became a community of faith, a nation listening to God. It was not so much that God loved Israel more than the other peoples of the earth, but somehow they were a people who learned how to listen to and hear the Word of God.

The experienced and known love of God set this people free. The books of the Bible which reflect their experience of God in their lives make up what we call the Old Testament. The *Tanach*, as it is called in Hebrew, consists of 46 books. These writings show an evolutionary development, a gradual coming to see how God acts in human life. As we go through the Scriptures, what we see in Israel's growth as a people is a pattern of what happens to every person and to every people who set out on the journey of faith. They go through stages and gradually come to see how God loves them and what God's liberation does for them.

Protestants refer to some of our Old Testament books as "apocryphal," as Jewish writings which are not really a part of Sacred Scripture. The books that they include in the Apocrypha are the first and second books of Maccabees, Tobias, Judith, Esther, Wisdom, Sirach, Baruch and parts of Daniel. Some Christians, therefore, have a shorter Old Testament, but in essence the Word is the same for all of us, both Catholics and Protestants. The basic message is the same no matter which version of the Bible we accept.

In addition to these Jewish Scriptures, all Christians accept as part of the Bible what we call the New Testament, that new Word which is personified and revealed to us in Jesus. The New Testament consists of 27 books, which were probably written over a period of about a 100 years. The Old Testament reflects an experience of about 2,000 years, so all together we have approximately a 2,100-year record of people learning to hear the Word of God.

This experience, this hearing and responding to the Word, moreover, is normative for understanding and interpreting that same ongoing dialogue today. We believe that the writers of Scripture were truly listening to the Lord, and so we call the Bible "inspired by God." We believe that the Lord was truly speaking to the scriptural authors, and that this inspired dialogue between God and humankind still continues in those who know how to trust and to listen. In other words, the experience of ancient Israel is our norm for today. It gives us the proper attitude for interpreting our salvation history.

Our faith, therefore, is not in the words of the Bible. That would be fundamentalism. Our faith is in a person. Our faith is in the Lord who is revealing himself to us. He is the Word who is calling us into personal dialogue. Fundamentalism is a slavish idealization of words which inevitably leads to a rigid, closed-minded, dead-ended approach to the Bible. The Word calls us into a personal dialogue which, in many respects, is like Jacob's wrestling with the angel (Genesis 32:23-33). Only there, in that sort of personal involvement, do we come face-to-face with the mystery that is God.

It was in that experience that Jacob was named Israel, which means "strong against God." In that moment Jacob became Israel, and Israel became a people. The people came into being in that experience of wrestling with the mystery of God. Today, we become the new Israel when we involve ourselves in that same wrestling match. There are no easy answers. There are no simple answers. To believe that there are would be to deny the experience of humanity.

We are called to walk the journey. And, pilgrim, there are no roads. Roads are made by walking. It is only in walking the journey that we come to know the answers. They are not always neat answers. They are not always "head" answers. They are most often "gut" answers. They are meaning. They are life. For what we seek, what we need, and what the Lord promises, is meaning and life.

The end and purpose of the Scriptures is to share this good news, to give our lives this meaning. The Bible does not set out to be a history book. It does not set out to teach science. It is not an answer book to all the practical problems of life. It purports to teach us religious truth—that is, truth about who God is and about how we relate to one another. We cannot expect anything more from the Scriptures, and we cannot criticize them for not being what they do not pretend to be. They do give us what we most basically need: that bread by which we truly live, the Word of the Father.

It is vital to realize that no single passage of the Bible can be taken in isolation from the others. In a sense, the first books of the Bible were not really completed until the last book was written. Each book has to be read in the context of all the others in order to be properly understood. If we do not do that, we inevitably sink into fundamentalism, that habit of basing too much on single phrases and isolated sentences. The fact is this: If we simply go searching after phrases, we can prove anything we want from the Scriptures. In order to interpret each passage properly, the whole thrust of the Bible must be known and understood. That is why it is so important to come to grips with the subject of this book, the great biblical themes which bring it all together.

In seeing that whole vision, in entering into that personal

dialogue, we experience the power of God's Word. The author of the Letter to the Hebrews tells us that the Word of God is something alive and active, that it cuts like a sharp sword which can slip through the place where the soul is divided from the spirit like the joint from the marrow of the bone. The Word can judge our secret emotions and thoughts, for everything is transparent to the One to whom we are ultimately accountable (Hebrews 4:12-13). If you go to the Scriptures seeking an onlooker's knowledge of God, you will never grow in true knowledge of God. If you stand back from the Scriptures like a cool critic and force the Word to prove itself in your life, you will never know its power to change your life.

The Bible was written in faith and it can be understood only in faith. We must seek first the Kingdom. We must allow ourselves to be children. We must ask for the gift of the Spirit. When we approach the Bible with this kind of faith, the words leap off the page and the Word speaks to our heart.

Franciscan theology tells us that love precedes knowledge. We truly know only that which we love. When we stand back analyzing and coolly calculating, we can never truly come to know anything. It is only in stepping out and giving ourselves to a person or to an experience or to a word that the person or experience or word can speak to us. You have to make that leap of faith, that act of love, that act of self-gift if you want to hear the Word of God speaking to you.

I cannot prove to you with any kind of logic or by any bit of philosophy that the Bible is, in fact, the Word of God. But I call you to step out and trust, to listen and say, "Lord, if you are in fact the Lord, then show yourself in my life and speak to my heart." Only when we have trusted God, put him first and allowed him to be the Lord, have we in fact known the power of his Word. Only then have we seen power in our lives.

It is so hard for us as educated and sophisticated, scientific and technological people to come to know the power of the Word of God. One reason for this is that we cannot let go. We do not really trust and believe that the Lord will speak to us, and so we remain forever outside of the dialogue. The ancient Hebrews, on the other hand, were people who knew how to enter into that dialogue. They were able to see the Lord in all of his creation, in all of their history and in all of their life.

Today, in order for us to be good Christians, we have to first become good Jews. We have to learn how to think as Jews, as Israelites, as Hebrews. As Pope Pius X said, we are spiritual Semites. In order to hear what the Scriptures are really saying, we have to develop that Semitic attitude toward creation, that biblical vision of history, that existential outlook on life which our Hebrew ancestors had. Then, in the Word of God, the universal patterns of human experience are revealed and given meaning. We see our own heart revealed. We see the pattern of our own lives, of our own communities of faith—yes, of the whole world—revealed. The great patterns, the basic patterns of life, are revealed in the Word of God.

When we enter into this dialogue with the Word of God, we find that it is forever new. It is forever leading us deeper. This is why we can read those words again and again, and each time they speak to us with new depth because each time we are at a new place. When truth is no longer new, someone once said, it is no longer the truth.

To arrive at a biblical mentality, we must first see what the Hebrews meant by faith. As they understood it, faith is always faith in a person, and a person is a union of head and heart and will. Consequently, faith is a totally personal response to another person. It is not a head trip. It is not something intellectual. That does not mean faith is anti-intellectual or irrational, but it does mean that head knowledge is only a part of it. Faith is not simply a matter of believing true ideas. It is a totally personal experience.

There is an old Catholic saying that even the devil *knows* the truth. The devil knows the doctrines and creeds of the Church, if we can put it that way. But that has nothing to do with faith. Faith is not intellectual assent to true statements. It is not simply accepting ideas and saying, "I believe this, I believe that." The devil can know true ideas, but he does not for one minute trust the Lord or hope in the Lord.

The kind of faith that Yahweh taught Israel was, quite simply, hope and trust. He invited them to put their hope and trust in him, believing that they would not be disappointed. And so they came to expect God's action in their life. They had

10

an expectant faith, and they allowed God to step into their life and to speak to them. People of faith like Abraham and Moses somehow heard the promise of the Lord in their lives, just as you and I must hear it.

Perhaps they didn't hear voices or see visions any more than you or I do. But somehow they knew the call of the Lord. They heard the Word of the Lord. They experienced the gift of the Lord and they received the gifts of the Lord.

And they never doubted their gift. They were willing to outstare the darkness and to wait for the promise to be fulfilled. For the Hebrew people, history was always a time between promise and fulfillment. They stood in the middle, waiting for the Word of the Lord to be realized, to be made real. And ever since then people of faith have continued to be the ones who outstare the void and know that somehow, some way, out of all this absurdity and meaninglessness and aimlessness, God's promise will be fulfilled.

The Hebrews were the only people of their time who had a sense that history was going somewhere. History had a direction; it was not the eternal return. Time was going in a straight line; it was not going around in circles and leading nowhere. Life was leading them somewhere; it was not a meaningless repetition. They had this vision because they saw the purposeful activity of God in their life. They experienced his providence, and they stood on that. They based their whole life on the awareness that God was good, that he was in fact the Lord, that he was leading them somewhere, and that his love for them was everlasting.

But sometimes they lost this vision and the prophets had to remind them of it. They were not allowed to pretend. They could not simply play religious games such as formalistic worship. When they watered down the Good News of God's love, when they lost sight of the direction in which it was leading them, God sent prophets like Isaiah to tell them they were missing their call:

Because this people
approaches me only in words,
honours me only with lip service

11

while its heart is far from me,
and my religion, as far as it is concerned, is
nothing but human commandment, a lesson
memorized.... (Isaiah 29:13 JB)

That prophetic word is frightening when we realize how much of our religion has been precisely that: human commandment, a lesson memorized—shades of the Baltimore Catechism!

And yet God is not dismayed. The Lord is not turned off when we do that. Look at his beautiful answer in the continuation of that same verse. He says, "...very well, I shall have to go on being prodigal of prodigious prodigies with these people." He is saying, in other words, "I shall have to go on pouring out my love in surprising and wondrous fashion. When they do not love me, I'm going to love them more. I'm going to lead them into a more beautiful future, if only they will allow me."

Throughout their history the Israelites experienced the unconditional, unrelenting love of God. Even when they did not obey the commandments, even when they did not believe that the Lord had new life for them, he gave it to them anyway. And so they came to see that new life does not depend on their obedience. Little by little they discovered that worthiness is not the issue. The ony real issue in life is the steadfast love of God. And the only real difference in people is between those who can believe this and those who cannot.

The good news always points to the future, to some place new, to the promised land. It never points backward. Yet the irony of Christian history has been our habit of looking backward and saying, "Back then was when we had miracles. Back then was when God was God, and when the great prophets lived. Back in the Middle Ages was when there were great saints..." Ironically, the Word of God was made into a conservative force rather than a liberating force. Because we were not truly listening to the Word of God, we did religious gymnastics and we lost touch with the power of God's Word.

The good news is that the Lord always calls us out of our own idol-making and our own insecurities to the security that he will give us, to the future that he will create. Christianity, like Judaism, is essentially a forward-looking religion because it calls us to destroy our idols, our defense mechanisms, and it leads us to trust in God alone. His love gives us the security to be insecure, to let go of the present and head toward the future.

The job of the prophets was to continually preach this new Word to the people, and to remind them to always expect something more. In the days of the prophet Amos, the Israelites (like ourselves) were losing the vision that had been given them. He prophesied that a day would come when they would not listen to the Lord and when they would not know where they were going:

> The time is coming, says the Lord Yahweh,
> when I will send famine on the land. It will not
> be a food famine or a water drought. It will be
> an inability to hear the word of God. People will
> wander east and west, north and south, looking
> for the word of God. They will seek everywhere,
> but they will not find it. (Amos 8:11-12)

The last 400 years there has been such a famine in the Church. We have believed that we do not need the Word of God, and we have lost our power. If we in the Church have lost our vitality, it is because we have not based our spirituality on the Scriptures, we have not allowed the Lord to build the Church on the Word of God.

This book called the Bible is the constitution of our Church, and yet there are Catholics who know nothing about it. The Scriptures mean nothing to them. They say the Old Testament is speaking about a different world than the one they know, or that the New Testament is talking about something else than what they are familiar with. But if the Scriptures do not speak to our hearts, it is because we have not had the real Christian experience yet. If the Lord is not speaking to us, we have not yet entered into dialogue with that Lord.

So I invite you again to open your heart to the Word of the Scriptures. Allow yourself to listen to the Lord, and the Lord will speak to you. It can make all the difference, but you have to want it. You have to seek it with all your heart. You have to seek first the Kingdom of God, and everything else will be given to you. I promise you that you will not be disappointed, for as the psalm says, no one who trusts in the Lord is ever disappointed.

Such is the call which the Word extends to us. Such is the general invitation of the Scriptures. But to appreciate how that call came to Israel and what in particular God invites us to, it is important to understand something about the various books which make up the Bible.

The Books of the Bible

The first portion of the Bible is called the *Pentateuch*, from the Greek words meaning "five books." This portion in Hebrew is called the *Torah*, the Law, and it can be found enthroned in every Jewish synagogue even today. These five books are not necessarily the oldest books of the Bible, but they do tell us how everything began. Genesis, for example, is the first book of the Bible, but it was not the first one written. It is a return to the beginnings in the light of the present, and it was actually composed perhaps as late as 500 B.C.

The second book of the Bible is Exodus, but in many ways this is the real beginning. It tells about the escape of the Hebrews from Egypt, and the stories of that adventure are probably some of the oldest narratives in the Bible.

Leviticus and Numbers are books which have a good deal of history in them, as well as laws and genealogies. We sometimes do not find this very meaningful. The Israelites, however, knew their history was significant because they saw God acting in and changing their history. In the same way, they came to see the laws that they needed to be a people as divine commands, as God-given. Today, of course, we do not feel bound to obey these multitudinous laws, and yet they are included in the Bible, in the inspired Word of God. This shows how very naturally we have come to recognize different levels of meaning and different ways of understanding the Word of God.

14

Deuteronomy, the fifth book of the Pentateuch, can be read as a beautiful account of God's love forming the Hebrews into a people. When you read the Book of Deuteronomy, you should allow the Hebrew spirit, the Jewish spirituality, to speak to you.

After the Pentateuch come the "historical books," but you must realize that none of these books are history as we understand it today. These books record the Israelites' experience of God's action in their life, reflected on and written down hundreds of years later. Perhaps they elaborated a bit, as people do when they write religious epics. But they had no reason to lie about their history. Why should they? The amazing thing is that they so often put themselves down, describing themselves as two-faced and unfaithful to Yahweh. This is because the purpose of these writings was not to set down an accurate record of Israel's history but to glorify God, whom they experienced as freeing them from slavery and leading them to a new land.

The books of Joshua and Judges recount how Yahweh helped the Israelites to conquer the promised land. We have to admit that there is a lot in these books which might disturb us—for example, the Israelites' hatred for the Canaanites. But we have to remember that the Israelites were at an earlier level of moral development, and at least they heard and responded to the Word that was spoken to them at that level.

In the books of Samuel, Kings, Chronicles, Ezra, Nehemiah and Maccabees, we find stories of religious heroes—no doubt glamorized, but each one making a point. And the main point they make is this: God is constantly working with them and for them; he is in their experience and influencing their lives.

The books of Ruth, Tobias, Judith and Esther give us additional stories of Jewish heroes and heroines. But what was it about these individuals that caused them to be looked upon as models, as persons to be imitated? When you get right down to it, it was their fidelity, their faithfulness to the God whom they experienced in their lives. Because the Israelites knew that God was faithful, fidelity was an important virtue to them, and so they respected and emulated faithful men and women.

The next group of writings are the "wisdom books." This collection includes the books of Job, Psalms, Proverbs, Wisdom and some others.

The Book of Job is set forth very much like a drama with a hero, Job, and a villain, Satan. It is a dramatic short story in which the protagonist hears the Word of the Lord and is gradually drawn into the mystery of God.

After that we have the Book of Psalms, 150 religious songs of the Hebrew people. Many of these beautiful prayers are still apropos for the prayer of Christians today.

The Book of Ecclesiastes is one which you might not want to read when you are feeling down. It's a bit pessimistic—and we might even call it cynical in spots—but it does show how we experience God during those negative moments in our lives. It relativizes all would-be absolutes.

Some people read the Song of Songs and blush. They cannot imagine why a book such as this would be in the Bible! But this just serves to show us how prudish and Victorian the Christian religion has become. The Israelites were not ashamed to compare our relationship with God to the sexual passion of a man for a woman and a woman for a man. There was nothing prudish about the Israelites; they were earthy, real, flesh-and-blood people.

In the books of Proverbs and Ecclesiasticus we see how people who were listening to the Lord came to some wise human conclusions. These writings give us a very down-to-earth, commonsense approach to God and to the world. And yet this is not the whole vision. We can never be satisfied with the practical insights of the wisdom books because the Lord leads us far beyond that human wisdom. Nevertheless, the knowledge which is communicated in these writings is an important beginning in religious understanding. We can perceive divine wisdom shining through them and recognize them as the inspired Word of God.

The last major division of the Old Testament contains "the prophets": Isaiah, Jeremiah, Lamentations, Baruch, Ezekiel, Daniel, Hosea, Joel, Amos, Obadiah, Jonah, Micah, Nahum, Habakkuk, Zephaniah, Haggai, Zechariah and Malachi. Each of the prophets was sent at a certain period of time to speak to Israel and to call the people back to a right relationship with God. Among these writings there are also stories of prophets who perhaps never existed as historical persons, but Israel nonetheless heard the Lord speaking through these people when it recalled their stories. Jonah and Daniel are two such prophetic figures in the Old Testament.

What we call the New Testament consists of 27 books, probably all written by about 100 A.D. Taken together, the New Testament writings articulate the new Word which God spoke to Israel and to the whole human world in and through Jesus Christ, the incarnate Word.

We are of course most familiar with the four Gospels. These are not biographies as we would understand that term today, but four different experiences of Jesus written down in four unique ways. Notice that Matthew does not call Luke a heretic because Luke says different things about Jesus, and Mark does not call John unorthodox because John speaks differently of Jesus. Rather, each author touches upon the mystery which is Jesus, and each one uncovers a bit of that mosaic which is the face of Christ.

Together these four evangelists invite you to a personal experience of the Word that is Jesus, similar to the experience which led them to write their own words about Jesus. The evangelists call you to be evangelized, to incarnate the good news in your own experience, to write your own life in Christ, to write the gospel according to Frank or Bill or Susan or Beth.

The Acts of the Apostles is something like a sequel to Luke's Gospel. It might well be called the Gospel of the Holy Spirit, the good news of what God can do when people let him into their lives and communities. It recalls those first days when the disciples experienced the power of the risen Jesus, and it describes the growth of the early Christian community.

After that come the epistles, or letters, of St. Paul written to the Romans, Corinthians, Galatians, Ephesians, Philippians, Colossians, Thessalonians and other communities and individuals in the early Church. Paul never knew Jesus in the flesh but he walked with him in the Spirit. In this respect Paul's experience is so similar to our own that his words can often speak directly to our own heart. Paul's life was transformed by

17

Jesus, and we can see that transformation occur, so that he can finally say that he lives no longer, but Christ lives in him (Galatians 2:20).

We are not really sure who wrote the Letter to the Hebrews, but that is not important. What is important is the way it reveals another aspect of the mystery of Jesus. The Letter of James, the two letters of Peter, the three letters of John and the Letter of Jude are all very short, and yet each in its own way adds a piece to the giant mosaic which shows us the face of Christ in the life of his body, the Church.

The Bible ends with the Book of Revelation, or the Apocalypse as it is sometimes called. It is for many people a very confusing book, but it is the book which finally draws the whole Bible together. You can perhaps best think of it as paradise revisited. Just as Genesis began with that first vision of a garden, so in the end we return to a garden. In the period between the two gardens, we see people trying to build a city of God, trying to create the kingdom of Israel, trying to establish the true Jerusalem. But in the end, after all the thousands of years of history, after all the blood and guts have been spilled, after all of the absurdity and the meaninglessness and the waiting and the hoping, we see that the Lord finally grants the new Jerusalem as a gift. He creates a new heaven and a new earth.

The apocalyptic vision of the Book of Revelation is this: In the end, all things are gifts. Every good thing that we have is something that we receive. It comes to us as gift, and because it is a gift it has the power to be redemptive. The relationship of giftedness redeems the world for us. It is in the relationship of receiver to giver that we are set free.

This is why I urge you, as you read these words, to allow the Scriptures to be gift for you. In reading the chapters of this book, and in reading the books of the Bible, allow God to be gracious to you. Allow him to be gift for you, because in that experience of his graciousness you will be set free.

Grace is everything. Grace is everywhere. From beginning to end—from Genesis to Revelation, we might say—this is the Word that the Lord is trying to communicate to us: that God is gift and we have to learn how to receive gifts. Once we hear this, nothing can be the same again.

18

CHAPTER TWO

Exodus:
The Journey of Faith

The journey of Exodus, the journey that Israel walked, is an image of the journey that every person makes when he or she sets out to follow the Lord. Israel is, as it were, humanity personified, and so what happened to Israel is what happens to everyone who sets out on the journey of faith.

The Escape From Egypt

In the Book of Exodus, Egypt is the place of slavery and the promised land is the place of freedom. The journey from Egypt to the promised land—through the Red Sea to Sinai and across the desert—is a saga which symbolizes our own struggle from slavery to freedom, once we have chosen to follow the Lord. The story of Israel symbolically describes the experience of our own liberation by God.

Until we look at Exodus as a symbolic story of religious truth, much of it seems distant and unreal. The events are either downright incredible or we have to believe that things were different then: God worked wonders for the Israelites, but he does not work that way any more.

The fact is, however, that God has not changed; it is people who have changed. The Israelites saw Yahweh acting in their lives. Their religious insight was really a product of religious hindsight: They reflected on their experience and they interpreted it in a new way. Today, on the other hand, we do not usually look back on what has happened and see the hand of God in it.

When that hindsight becomes foresight—when it becomes a hope and expectation that God will do in the future what he did in the past—we call that the vision of faith. It is precisely this vision that is essential for authentic worship. In liturgy we recall the wonderful works of God through the reading of the Scriptures and, having done so, we see the Lord's presence in the midst of our own lives. Very likely the exciting Exodus stories were told and retold in liturgical worship before they were ever written down. They are some of the oldest sections of the Bible (for example, see Exodus 15:1-21).

The stories of Exodus make religious sense to people only to the extent that they are converted, only to the degree that they are walking the journey of faith. If you are walking in the Spirit and listening to the Spirit, you can relate these stories to your own life, you can identify with the experience of Israel. The person who is alive in the Spirit can recognize spiritual things. If, on the other hand, you are playing a social game called religion or an academic game called theology, this book will never speak to you.

Without that moment of conversion, or that desire for conversion, people are the way Jesus described them: "They have eyes but they do not see. They have ears but they do not hear" (Mark 8:18). To receive the wisdom of the Scriptures, therefore, we have to be open to the Spirit. We have to turn to the Lord and let him lead us on the journey of faith. We have to be willing to experience the Exodus in our own lives, to let the Lord take us from slavery to freedom, from Egypt to Canaan, knowing that between Egypt and Canaan is the desert.

The original Exodus experience, the escape of the Hebrews from slavery in Egypt, happened somewhere between 2000 and 1200 B.C. We do not know the exact date. We do not even know if those who escaped were all related to each other, if they were really a "people." Scripture scholars tell us that very likely they were a hodgepodge of individuals who were enslaved together. What formed them into a people, what gave them a common identity, was the Exodus experience. They were led out of Egypt by the faith of one man, and that man was Moses.

Who was this Moses?

He appears to have been a well-educated man who rose to some degree of prominence in Egypt even though he himself was probably not an Egyptian. In the early chapters of Exodus we read that he committed a murder. He saw someone harassing one of the slaves, so he killed the man and buried him in the sand. When Moses was found out, he ran away. A few years later, he had what we would call a religious experience. He felt himself being called to go back to Egypt to free the oppressed and enslaved.

In the story of Moses we can see a pattern which we find so often in the Scriptures. The Lord gets one person to listen to him, and then he uses that person to lead his people forward on the journey of faith. As it turns out, Moses is not a good speaker. He stutters, and he is afraid that the people will laugh at him. But the Lord usually chooses unlikely subjects to be his instruments. He picks the little people, the common and sometimes even contemptible people (1 Corinthians 1:28) so that they cannot glory in themselves. They know for sure that they are not doing it; it is the Lord who is doing it through them.

In the beginning, therefore, Moses is a fugitive with a speech impediment. Yet God singles Moses out. His experience of God is symbolized in the story of the burning bush. God is radiant and alive, the fire hidden inside of form, a flame that never goes out. (Exodus 3:1ff) After God reveals himself, he gives Moses the task for which he has chosen him: "I am sending you to Pharaoh to bring my people, the children of Israel, out of Egypt" (Exodus 3:10).

At this, Moses balks, and he asks God how in the world he is supposed to accomplish this. The Lord replies, "I shall be with you" (Exodus 3:12). He does not tell Moses how to do it; he does not give him directions or a timetable.

And that's the way it always is in the Scriptures. God simply says, "I'll be with you," and that's all. God is saying, in effect, "I will do it. Trust me." Nothing more than that. Moses' power is the presence of the Lord, and the directions come as he walks the journey. This will be borne out again as the Hebrews go through the desert, and it remains the pattern for the person of faith today. There is a certain bias toward risk and action. Otherwise faith becomes mystified and self-protective, as it does in much religion.

So Moses takes the risk. All that God has given him is a promise, and yet he acts on that promise. The person of faith is the one who expects the promise to be fulfilled; history for that person becomes a time between promise and fulfillment. Such a person depends on that promise, listening and waiting, hoping and trusting, and acting. It is a way of tremendous self-discipline, a way that the world does not know. As Jesus said, the way is narrow, and there are few who want to take it (Matthew 7:14). It is the way of faith.

On the basis of this promise, Moses tells the people that they are going to be set free. Now, why should they believe him? Why should they think that this man could lead them out of slavery into freedom? But he talks with them, he prays with them, and finally the people are convinced: "The people believed, and when they heard that the Lord was concerned about them and had seen their affliction, they bowed down in worship" (Exodus 4:31). We see in this episode the classic response to the good news: When we first hear the message of God's love, we don't believe it; then, when we start to believe it, it suddenly looks like all our problems are over. It is the surge of strength that comes with accepting the vision. It seems that nothing can get in the way, that nothing can stop us.

But of course it can, and it does. In this story, the obstacle is the hardness of Pharaoh's heart and the securities of the system. But Moses confronts this established evil with the power and resistance of God. In Exodus 7—14 we read about the 10 plagues which Yahweh visited upon Egypt, including the final one which convinces Pharaoh to let the Hebrews go free.

Biblical scholars today suggest that the plague stories are perhaps based on natural occurrences. For example, the Nile overflowed every year and the country was overrun by frogs whenever this happened. Similar explanations are possible for the water turning red, and for most of the other plagues. Still, from the perspective of faith, even these natural phenomena became events through which God was working to get the Hebrews out of Egypt. And when the stories got written down hundreds of years after the events, they were embellished by centuries of telling and retelling. Yet the undeniable fact remains: Some slaves in the most powerful empire of the ancient world were allowed to go free. God freed the oppressed! This itself was a miracle, and the stories of the plagues served to underline the miraculousness of what happened.

The same could be said about the crossing of the Red Sea, with "the wall of water on each side." Whether or not this is the exact way it happened is not important. It could have happened this way, but our faith is not based on passages such as this one being literally true. That again would be fundamentalism, which is faith in words rather than faith in a person. Israel's faith was in the Lord, and so is ours.

Scholarly research indicates that the escaping Hebrews probably crossed the Sea of Reeds, a swampy area in the northern part of the Red Sea. The runaway slaves were able to pass through on foot, but the Egyptians in their heavy chariots got mired down in the mud. The important thing is this: When the Hebrews reached the other side of the sea or swamp or whatever, they were free and the Egyptians were caught in the middle of it. The Hebrews saw this miraculous escape as engineered by Yahweh. Perhaps that is why, as the story was passed on from generation to generation, the miracle got bigger and bigger until the water was a wall 20 feet high on both sides.

This does not mean that we do not believe the Bible is the Word of God. We believe that God loved the Israelites and liberated them in every aspect of their lives. We believe that this is what the Bible is saying and that the rest may be embellishment. We believe that this is the Word which is eternally true. It is just as true today as it was then. God is always loving us and liberating us (in more ways than we are usually ready for!).

Sometimes it is only from hindsight that we recognize that God has been saving us. Sometimes it is only when we look back over the years that we see the providence of God. When we were traveling through those years, none of them may have seemed very glorious. But when we look back, we can see how God was leading us, and we behold his glory in our lives, the beauty of his saving love.

Yet when we are in the middle of it, it may not seem very beautiful at all. It may seem quite ordinary. Usually we cannot tell for certain that God is acting in our life. The way of faith is not a way of certitude.

I can imagine quite easily that Moses faltered on occasion. He must have hesitated and wondered whether God was really leading him, or whether he was just on some big ego trip. If Moses saw some visible apparition or heard some audible sounds which made him absolutely certain that he was right, Moses' way would not have been a way of faith. It would have been a way of knowledge.

We are all called to a way of faith. At each step God asks us to trust him, to say yes to him, to put our lives in his hands. It's like walking around in a pitch-dark room, afraid that we are going to bump into something or trip or fall. We put our hands out in front of us and walk very slowly. We want desperately to have our pathway illuminated. We want to know where we are going and how we are going to get there. A voice comes to us out of the darkness, asking us to trust. We want certitude, but instead God asks us to have faith.

Our faith, then, is in the Lord. Our trust is in him and not in our cleverness or our planning, not in our status or our money. In the darkness, all our securities are gone. In the desert, all our idols are taken away from us. The darkness, the desert, is the place for learning total dependence on God. It is the school of surrender.

Very often we experience faith in its purest form when we are in the midst of suffering. Those who are young in the Lord sometimes picture themselves suffering for him, being glorious martyrs. But actually, it's not glorious at all when you are in the middle of it. It seems so meaningless, and that's the heart of the suffering. The essence of the desert experience is that you want to get out. If you could find a pattern in it, it would have some meaning. If you could find some purpose in it, it would give you a sense of direction. But you can't, and so you suffer.

The Wandering in the Desert

The Israelites wandered in the Sinai desert for 40 years. They went around in circles and seemed to be going nowhere. Now and then they would find an oasis, a moment of relief, a place of life. Of course they would want to settle down and stay, but Moses would say, "No, pull up your tent pegs. We're going to a new land. It's out there, I promise." Understandably, the people would object: "Why should we believe you? It was better back in Egypt where we had three square meals a day. We have nothing here."

The temptation for anyone of us who starts out on the journey of faith is to turn back. We find ourselves saying, "It was easier in our old slavery. It was easier being bound by sins and lies. It was easier being an ordinary, middle-class American than walking the journey of faith." We want to go back to Egypt as much as the Israelites did. But the Lord calls us to remember in the darkness what we once saw in the light.

Every so often at times like that, in the middle of our desert, God grants us a moment of transfiguration, a moment of Sinai such as Moses experienced. For us as for him it can be a moment of grace, a religious experience in which the Lord is undoubtedly real. But after a while, as always, we have to come down from the mountaintop and walk in the desert. Then, a few days or a few weeks later, it all starts to seem a bit unreal. We wonder whether it was just our imagination, and we start to doubt the memory of what we experienced shortly before. This is exactly what the Israelites did, and Moses has to remind them again and again that God's love is not an illusion.

Still, the people complain that they are hungry: "If God is real, why doesn't he feed us?" So Moses prays to the Lord, and the Lord replies, "I will feed them. But I will feed them only enough food for a day at a time. I will let manna drop from heaven, but they are to pick up only enough to feed themselves for one day." Again we see the essential lesson of the desert, that the Lord wants us to trust him continually, day by day.

Some of the Israelites, of course, still refuse to learn that lesson. They want to store up the manna, to save for tomorrow. But the Lord says, "No! Take only enough for today. I will give you your food every day." It is with this in mind that Jesus taught us to pray, "Give us this day our daily bread."

How that goes against our grain! We always want to plan for the future, to take care of ourselves. But the Lord invites us to stop worrying about tomorrow, to surrender control, to trust him not only day by day, but even minute by minute.

The people who stepped out into the desert with Moses felt whole and strong, perhaps for the first time. You might expect that they would get stronger as they went along. But that is not what happened. Instead, they experienced weakness and weariness. There was division among the people. They discovered that they were not as whole and strong as they thought they were.

So often the same happens to us. When all of our idols are taken away from us—all of our securities, all of our defense mechanisms and safe explanations—then we find out who we really are. We are so little, so poor, so empty. In the desert the Lord takes our idols away from us, and we have to come before him poor and humble. In that encounter we discover who we are and who God is for us. Then we can let the Lord be our salvation. It is not our work but his, from beginning to end.

Thomas Merton once observed that there are many people who leave Egypt, but few of them ever enter the promised land. Most of us stop on the far shore of the Red Sea, afraid to step out into the desert. We have gone through the sea, the waters of Baptism, but now we sit there on the edge of the desert. We have experienced our dependence on God, but we do not want to experience total dependence on God—at least not at any real risk to ourselves. It seems that we can take only so much reality.

Just before they crossed the sea, Moses told the Israelites that there was nothing to be afraid of. And he told them what they had to do if they allowed themselves to be dependent on the Lord: "Have no fear! Just stand where you are, and you will see how Yahweh will save you. The Egyptians you see today will never bother you again. Yahweh will fight for you. All you have to do is keep still" (Exodus 14:13-14).

Today, those same words are directed at us: We need to

let go of fear, to be still, and to let God be God. The Lord will do the fighting for us, and he will give us the victory. Our job is simply to keep still and allow him to do the fighting. Like the Israelites, we need to put down our weapons of war, we need to put down our sword and shield and armor, we need to let go of our willfulness.

When they reached the other side of the Red Sea, Moses and the children of Israel sang this song to the Lord:

> I will sing to the Lord, for he has triumphed
> gloriously! Horse and chariot he has cast into
> the sea! The Lord is my strength, my courage,
> and my salvation. He is my God; I will praise
> him! He is the God of my father; I will extol him!
> The Lord is a warrior; Yahweh is his name.
> (Exodus 15:1-3)

There is one thing you should notice about this early liturgical song: It is pure praise. From beginning to end, it sings the praises of God. In contrast, enthusiastic praise is something that is almost entirely missing from our modern Church liturgies. We are uncomfortable with this kind of display of feeling. It does not fit in with our image of ourselves as proper and sophisticated. We resist it. We fight it. Why, we ask, does God need our praise?

The answer, of course, is that he doesn't. Praising God is good not because God needs it but because it is a beautiful thing to do. The truly wonderful things in life are not the necessities but the useless gifts. The greatest beauty happens in the totally unnecessary exchanges between lovers. In the midst of self-giving, love happens. In the milieu of gift-giving, grace happens.

Those who would ask if God needs our praise might also ask if God needs our worship. But the answer is the same. God does not need us in church on Sunday morning. He is not happier after we have sat there for 45 minutes. Our worship does not change God, and it is not meant to. Worship, especially Eucharistic worship, is meant to be a time of mutual self-giving, and a time of mutual gift-giving, an exchanging of desire.

27

In Sunday worship we, who have slowly surrendered our lives all week, come together to celebrate that life-giving. We give ourselves symbolically to the Lord, giving up our self-sufficiency by confessing our weakness, giving him our attention by hungering for his Word, seeing ourselves broken and poured out in the bread and the wine. In return, the Lord gives himself to us, giving us his healing forgiveness, giving us the wisdom of his Word, giving us the gift of his personal presence in the Eucharist, liberating us for *all* of life.

In that mutual sharing, something beautiful happens, something wonderful happens, something happens that is both human and divine. Unless that happens, nothing happens. Unless that happens, you are bored. Unless that happens, the words of the liturgy make no sense to you and worship is nothing more than ritualism.

Nor is there any substitute for entrusting your life to God, for putting your present and your future in his hands. Fussing around with the externals of liturgy is no replacement for interior worship. You can try to turn people on with banners, guitars, processions, or what have you, but you are naive if you believe in those gimmicks in themselves. Authentic worship is inspired by faith, not by frills.

That is partly the meaning of the golden calf, which comes later in the Exodus story. The Israelites lose touch with God, so they make a substitute which will help them feel religious. They bow down and worship something which is not God. They even get enthusiastic about it. But the truth is this: They have lost contact with the Lord; their excitement over the golden calf is just a cover-up for the divine-human interaction which is not happening.

But that's getting ahead of ourselves. We left the Hebrews on the bank of the Red Sea. At this point, they are very much aware of the presence and the power of God. They are in touch with who it is that saved them and how that liberation came about. And so, after they see the Egyptians defeated, after they experience the victory that God has given them, the Israelites "put their faith in Yahweh and in his servant, Moses" (Exodus 14:31). Notice it does not simply say they put their faith in God; they put their faith in God and in a human being just like them.

It is the same in our own day. Trust in the Lord has to go together with trust in other people. It cannot be just "God and me." Our relationship with the Lord teaches us how to love and trust others. But it is also true that our faith in other people supports our ability to have faith in God. The two work together, and working together they form us into a community. That's one reason why we call it a community of faith, and why we call our life together a faith life.

The faith life of a community is built on love and trust. In a Christian community it is built on faithfulness to God and to the others with whom we share the life of faith. The Israelite community was no different. They too had to be faithful if they were going to be a community, a people. The Ten Commandments, which are found in chapter 20 of the Book of Exodus, describe in essence how the Israelites were to be faithful to God and to one another.

The Ten Commandments

If you read the whole Book of Exodus, you find many more than 10 commandments. The Decalogue simply sums up all these innumerable laws; and these 10 can be still further reduced to two, as Jesus taught: love of God and love of neighbor, or fidelity to the Lord and fidelity to others. Those who accept the first three commandments say, in effect, that they will trust the Lord above all else. Those who accept the last seven commandments declare that they will trust one another.

The very first commandment in a way sums up all 10: "I am the Lord, your God. You shall have no others gods besides me." Biblically speaking, the only real sin is idolatry. Idolatry is making something a god that is not God. The biblical meaning of sin, in other words, is infidelity to what *is*, and infidelity to what is, is infidelity to God.

Now, if that's really the case, then I suspect that many people have never been guilty of sin, at least not in the biblical sense of that term. You cannot be unfaithful to a personal relationship until you first have one and, sadly, many people have never been involved in a personal relationship with God.

They have never personally experienced God loving them, nor have they themselves loved God; and so they cannot be unfaithful to a loving relationship with him.

This is not to suggest that people never do any wrong. People do lots of wrong things, lots of bad things. Perhaps they even bring much evil into their lives and into the world. But evil naturally tends to bring about evil, just as good naturally leads to good. If doing good is its own reward, then doing evil is its own punishment. People often commit evil, and they suffer the effects of evil in their lives. But I doubt that most people ever, in the biblical sense, commit sin.

We are called to a personal relationship with the Lord, just as Israel was. It was because Israel was unfaithful in her relationship with Yahweh that the prophets equated her sinfulness with prostitution. They called Israel a whore because she had known the love of the Lord and then turned her back on him. So unless we fall in love with God, we cannot sin. But once we experience and know God's love for us, then we are capable of sin. That personal relationship brings with it a new responsibility. We have a right to expect more from believers than from unbelievers.

Another dimension of that personal relationship is brought out by the third commandment, which tells us to keep holy the Lord's day. The Israelities were commanded to rest on the seventh day of every week. Everything was to stop; no one was to work. God wanted to teach them that the real power in their lives came from him. One day a week, a seventh of their time, they were to rest in the Lord. The sabbath was to be a day set aside to joyfully live out their dependence on God. As the psalm says, "This is the day that the Lord has made. Let us be glad and rejoice in it" (Psalm 118:24).

The sabbath rest is the Lord's way of teaching us that he is the real power in our lives. He says, in effect, "Just one day a week, stop achieving, stop accomplishing, stop doing anything that is task-oriented. On that day, let me do the achieving, let me do the saving." That is the real meaning of the third commandment: freedom from willfulness. It has nothing to do with rules about what kind of work you can or cannot do on Sunday. That legalistic interpretation over the centuries covered up the understanding which is at the heart of the biblical message.

If we look now to the last seven commandments, we see that they all have to do with relationships between individuals. They are the absolute minimums that have to be observed if people are going to live together in community, if they are really going to be a people. Children have to reverence and obey their parents. Married people have to avoid adultery. No one can be allowed to go around killing or stealing. Everyone has to be honest and tell the truth. We must curb our desires for *more*. Everyone, in other words, has to trust the others and trust the community. Trust is the foundation of peoplehood, fidelity is the foundation of unity.

These seven moral precepts express the fundamental ethics according to which most peoples have lived down through the ages. Yet the Israelites knew that these ethical demands came from God; for unless they heeded these words, they could not hear the deeper Word in their hearts.

Having received from God the Ten Commandments, their rule of life, the Israelites again set out across the desert. Yahweh was always with them, present in a pillar of fire by night and a pillar of cloud by day. He was leading them to the promised land, and yet they did not know where they were going. None of them had ever been there before. They had to trust the Lord. It was a journey into *un*certitude.

Not only that, but they also had to trust the Lord's timing. When the pillar moved, they moved. When the pillar stopped, they stopped, and they did not march forward again until God led them forward. Understandable frustrations arose.

We too want to get out of the desert. We always want to shorten the time, to get it over with. But we cannot rush the journey of faith. We have to attune ourselves to the timing of God, walking as God leads us.

An Image of Faith

The Book of Exodus gives us many images of faith: crossing the Red Sea, setting out into the desert, following the pillar of fire.

Perhaps there is yet another image which can give us a sense of what faith is all about. Although not found in the Scriptures, it captures the heart of biblical faith.

Picture, if you will, a stone table, and next to it a flying carpet. The table is solid; its legs are strong. The carpet is floating at the same height as the table top, but there is nothing underneath it. You look at the table, you look at the carpet, and the Lord says, "Come."

The table looks so safe. You can tell what you are standing on, you know where the edges are, you are sure you won't fall. So naturally, you head for the table. But the Lord says, "No, over here."

"On that, Lord?" you ask. "How do I know it will hold me up?"

The Lord insists, "I'm telling you, come over here."

"But, Lord," you protest, "there's nothing holding it up. How do I know it won't fall down?"

So the Lord assures you, "I have called you, and I'll sustain you. It is I who will hold you up."

Finally, reluctantly, you give in. "Well, okay, Lord, if you say so."

And so you test it out. You press on it and it looks like it goes down a bit. But it doesn't sink to the floor. So you summon all your courage, and you climb onto the carpet.

Suddenly, you're floating! You feel so alive! You know for sure the Lord is loving you. You can hardly contain your joy. "Wow, Lord! Why didn't I believe you? If I had listened to you sooner, I could have been reborn! I would have known what it means to live! Oh, thank you, Lord!"

But then, it gets a little windy. You wonder what's happening. "Lord, stop it," you plead. But God doesn't stop it.

The wind blows harder, and you find yourself wondering whether you're really so safe. You look around, and you notice that the Lord has started pulling out the threads from the carpet!

Right away, you jump onto the stone table, and you feel a lot safer. But then you hear the Lord calling. "What are you doing over there? I thought you were going to trust me. Didn't you say you would leave everything and follow me?"

"Yes, but…"

"All right, then, trust me. Let me take away all those things you think you need. I will give you freedom. I will make you a new creation. But you have to believe in me. You have to believe that I can do it."

"I do, Lord," you say defensively. "But please stop pulling those threads out!"

You meekly get back on the carpet. Once again you feel the excitement. Once again you feel the wind. Once again you look around and—wouldn't you know it? The Lord's at it again, pulling out the threads.

So there you are. The carpet is getting threadbare. The wind is getting gusty. That stone table looks so secure. You start bargaining. "Lord, why couldn't I stand on that? I would still be a good Christian. I wouldn't disobey the commandments. I'd still go to Mass on Sundays. I'd even give more money to the poor. It's too scary over here!"

But the Lord doesn't let you go. "Just trust me," he reassures you. "That's not where it's at. This is where life is. I will be your joy. I will be your hope. I will be your fullness."

"Okay, Lord," you say. And as the time goes on, you see the Lord continuing to pull out the threads until finally there is nothing left but him.

And that's exactly what God wanted you to see. That's exactly what you needed to experience for yourself. It was not the power of the carpet that sustained you, it was the power of the Lord.

In the end, you find that all you thought you were going to lose is given to you in abundance—30-, 60-, 100-fold, as the Gospel says—poured into your lap and overflowing (Luke 6:38).

The fulfillment that the Lord gives always surpasses our expectations. God will not be outdone in generosity. Whatever we let go of will be given back to us many times over. But we don't know that except through hindsight. When we first set out on the journey of faith, we don't know that.

The Book of Exodus ends with God still leading the people forward into history. It seems ironic, but Moses did not get to enter the Promised Land. He saw it from a distance, looking at it from across the Jordan, but he died without setting foot in Canaan.

Later generations of believers thought there should be some theological explanation for this, so they suggested that God punished Moses in this way for those times in the desert when he didn't trust God 100 percent. They gave an interpretation which fit their own experience of God, and apparently they experienced God as punishing and vindictive.

But that is not my own experience of God, and that is not the God I find in the Scriptures. To me, it makes more sense to believe that Moses did not have to set foot in the promised land because he was already walking in it. He was walking the journey of faith, he was living in the Kingdom. He had met the Lord on Mount Sinai, and so he did not have to go somewhere else to meet him. His journey was complete, even before it ended. We can see too that there was nothing on the west bank of the Jordan which was not also on the east bank. In a sense the journey was his destination.

God was constantly calling them to the promised land, but just as constantly they kept wanting to go in their own direction. By not trusting God with their whole hearts, they found themselves going around in circles. If they had believed with a firm and constant faith, their journey might have taken a lot less time. They could have walked straight across that desert into Canaan.

But instead, they doubted. Instead, they hesitated. Instead, they kept wanting to go their own way. They were tempted, just as you and I are tempted. You want to believe, but the good news sounds too good to be true. You want to trust, but you wonder whether the Lord will really hold up your flying carpet. And so your journey—whichever one you happen to be on at the moment—takes longer than it needs to take. But maybe there is no other way for us humans.

In spite of those doubts, in spite of those fears, the Lord's promise to you is still the same as it was to Israel, and the same as it was to Moses. Surrender to the Lord completely, and God will sustain you. God will feed you. God will give you life. God will fill your heart with love.

Like the Israelites, you will find that the desert is not all desert. The way to the promised land leads to life even in the midst of the desert. When you least expect it, there is an oasis.

As it says in the Scriptures, God will make the desert bloom (Isaiah 35:1).

Or like Moses, you may find that you do not have to arrive in order to arrive. God can give you the promised land even before you get there. You can live in the Kingdom even before the Kingdom comes. For if you seek the Kingdom of God above all else, everything else will be given to you besides.

CHAPTER THREE

Joshua to Kings:
The Ordinary Becomes
Extraordinary

This section of the Scriptures can seem rather complicated at first reading. In it you find leaders and people, kings and prophets doing so many things one after another that it is hard to get a hold of the big picture. There are a few fundamental themes running through this section, however, which weave the various events into a tapestry of salvation history.

Joshua, Judges, Ruth, Samuel and Kings are listed among the "historical books" of the Bible. They are not history, however, in the modern sense of that term. They are based on actual events, to be sure; but the stories they tell us come out of a long process of theological reflection on those events. The result is a religious epic in which the stories are simplified, the characters are idealized, and the events are exaggerated. For both the tellers and the hearers of these stories—for they were passed along by word of mouth for generations before being written down—the important element was not the details but the religious meaning. They were looking back on their path and seeing it illuminated by the way God had been true to his promises.

I can see a parallel to this process in the life of the New Jerusalem Community. For a number of years the Lord has been working miracles for us. Back in 1971, for example, he gave us a mansion to live in. I believe it had 32 rooms. Now I'd be willing to bet that when some of our young people tell children of their own about the early days of the community, the mansion will have grown a lot larger. Maybe by then it will have 50 or 100 rooms. And it will be even more impressive in appearance than it was to me when I first saw it. Why? Because they will be telling their children how they saw God acting in a big way in their lives. They will be communicating how impressed they were with the way the Lord was taking care of them. That's the truth the story conveys, not the architectural details of the mansion.

This is exactly what the Israelites did in passing down their stories to their children. Sometimes we read these stories, however, and we find them hard to believe. But that's our problem 25 centuries later; it wasn't their problem. Why should they want to tell lies? They were trying to communicate how God was real to them, how he worked in their lives. We can see how honest they were because they were not afraid to show their own ancestors in a bad light from time to time. They preserved a history which criticized the nation for not following the Lord, for bowing down before false idols. If they wanted to whitewash the past, the Israelites would certainly have painted a more glamorous picture of themselves.

Joshua

The Book of Joshua begins with the Israelites being led across the River Jordan to the promised land. The Lord reassures them of his promise to be with them; all they need to do to conquer the land is to trust in his presence (Joshua 1:9).

What follows next seems very ordinary. Joshua sends scouts to spy on the Canaanites across the river. Meanwhile, the people in camp get ready for the final crossing. Here we are at the beginning of this momentous chapter in salvation history, and there is nothing very special about it!

It is exactly the same with us. Our daily life seems so ordinary while we are going through it. Very often it is only by looking back over our inglorious past that we begin to discern that something truly glorious was happening. In the same way the Israelites in real life probably went through these apparently unspiritual events and only later, looking back on them, began to discover their spiritual meaning.

For example, one of the spiritual themes which emerges through the ordinary events in this section of the Scriptures is *monotheism*. Authentic monotheism is not an abstract belief that there is one God rather than many gods "up there." It is a concrete confidence in one God "down here" who offers real salvation, as opposed to the many false gods in our lives who offer empty promises. The Israelites, as we shall see, had a hard time with this concrete confidence in one God. They could not believe that Yahweh would really save them, and so they were always trying to make alliances with other nations instead of trusting in the Lord.

We ourselves can say that we are authentic monotheists only when we put our faith in the one God who *is*, instead of selling out to lesser gods who cannot save. When we look back over our lives, then, we see that pattern of faith emerging over the course of our lives, and we can see how the Lord was acting even when every action seemed so ordinary.

Just before the Israelites are about to cross the Jordan into the promised land, however, Joshua tells the people to do something extraordinary. He tells them to make themselves holy: "Sanctify yourselves, because tomorrow Yahweh will work wonders among you" (Joshua 3:5). The idea here is sacrifice, from the Latin words *sacrum facere*, which mean "to make holy." The right meaning of sacrifice has little to do with suffering, which is often the connotation we give to it. The biblical concept of sacrifice has everything to do with trusting in God. It is entering wholly into a holy state of confidence that God can provide us with what we are giving up.

Let's say, for example, that you are hooked on cigarettes. But at a certain point in your life you ask yourself, "Why do I need this artifical stimulation?" So you turn in confidence to the Lord, asking God to give you real stimulation, real vitality in your life. As a sign that you are trusting God to supply your needs now, you give up smoking. It is quite possible to get in touch with the strength the Lord can give you by surrendering something on which you have been depending for strength—a false god.

Sacrifice, then, is not primarily a method of physical

deprivation but a means of spiritual growth. It is with this in mind that Joshua tells the people to fill themselves up with the Lord today, and to be ready to see miracles tomorrow.

And what happens on the next day? The first thing that happens is that they cross the Jordan the same way they crossed the Red Sea: The water stops flowing and the people march on dry land (Joshua 3:13-17). The author here uses the same literary device as the author of Exodus: He tells a miracle story to communicate the miraculousness of the event. In doing so, he also conveys the idea that they get across the river not on their own power but on God's power. And, of course, in retrospect it truly is miraculous that this band of runaway slaves would cross the Jordan with the hope of conquering Canaan—and succeed!

How they succeeded seems puzzling to us, if not downright revolting. They defeated the local armies, killed any survivors and burned their cities to the ground. Strange as it seems, this was in fact an advance over a more primitive morality in which conquered peoples were tortured, their women raped, their children enslaved and their possessions looted. Instead, the Israelites were told to go into a town and put it "under a ban," that is, to consecrate it and set it aside for the Lord. The Israelites were not allowed to enslave the people or steal their property for their own use. Instead, the town had to be destroyed and offered in sacrifice to the Lord.

What we see here is a good example of how God always meets people where they are and calls them forward, one step at a time. Yahweh did not ask Israel to abide by the just war theory or the principles of nonviolence. He asked them instead not only to refrain from raping and looting and enslaving, but to offer it all up to him. In this way they could learn that they did not have to depend on those things in order to be happy. It was a slow, evolutionary growth in morality.

We should not be surprised. We who are Catholics have gone through that same evolutionary growth in faith. Not long ago we believed that since we were God's new chosen people, he was with us and not with anyone else. God was in our church and not in any other churches. We didn't have to like Protestants; in fact, they were heretics, and so they were our enemies.

Recently, however, the Lord has led us beyond that more primitive stage of faith. He is leading us beyond our initial narrowness to see that other Christians are our brothers and sisters in the Lord. Today God wants us to more fully recognize how unconditional his love is. What we witness in the Book of Joshua is merely an earlier stage in the slow, sometimes painful, evolutionary growth in the understanding of where he is leading his people.

In the sixth chapter of this book, we are told about the fall of the city of Jericho, but we must remember that the story as we have it was written at a much later date. The original account has obviously passed through a great deal of literary development. Modern archaelogists tell us that the walls of that city had fallen long before Joshua ever got there. But the biblical author uses the reality of the fallen walls to create a story of extraordinary confidence in the power of God.

Yahweh tells the Israelites that he is going to deliver Jericho and its king into their hands, but the battle plan he gives them is supremely impractical. They are to parade around the city walls for six days in complete silence, carrying the ark of the covenant. On the seventh day they are told to march around in silence, but to shout when they hear a trumpet blast. When the trumpet sounds, the people shout, and of course the walls come tumbling down. What appeared to be impractical turns out to be supremely practical.

The point of the story is this: There is a different way to fight battles. The Lord is teaching them a whole new way to win over evil. The Quakers discovered this method in the Bible long ago and called it the Lamb's War, using an image from the Book of Revelation. The idea is to let the Lord go to battle for you, to let the Lord do the fighting. Today we are slowly coming to understand this necessary theology of nonviolence and peacemaking. We hope it is not too late.

There is a passage in 2 Chronicles which also conveys this idea beautifully. In chapter 20 a prophet tells the Israelites, who are confronted by a mighty army, that they should follow the Lord's battle plan if they want to see the enemy defeated. When they ask the prophet how they are to fight, he doesn't tell them to put the archers or the spear carriers in the front line.

No, he tells them to put singers out in front! So their army marches into battle led by a front line singing the praises of the Lord. The enemy is thrown into confusion, and the Israelites win without even trying. True spirituality is supremely creative.

All this sounds so unreal and naive, and yet it is so very applicable to us today. What do we want to do when we are faced with a Jericho in our own life? We see those huge walls, and we want to take them by storm. We see those stubborn obstacles, and our common sense tells us to use everything within our power against them. But the Lord says there is a new kind of power that we should use instead. It is the power of nonviolence, the power of love, the power of truth.

In Leonard Bernstein's *Mass*, there is a piece which sings of the Word of the Lord. It begins quietly, then builds in strength over 30 or 40 lines of music. It says that the Word of the Lord cannot be imprisoned, it cannot be scuttled, it cannot be abolished. Like the music in this piece, the Word of the Lord is growing, it is moving forward, it is winning.

The Lord's Word is powerful because it speaks of something real, even though it is hard to believe in at first. It is the power of God's love, slowly but steadily working its way into human history and transforming it.

The patience of God is impressive. He has waited thousands of years of Hebrew history and thousands of years of Christian history for his love to bear fruit. We see so little of it in the world around us, yet the vision of faith lets us see that, little by little, it is winning. The Word of the Lord is showing its power, and it is going to be victorious. It will overcome the Jerichos in our lives, and it will overcome the armies of the world as well.

In Joshua's time the power of God overcame the armies of the Canaanites one by one, and eventually the Israelites were about to portion out the promised land among the 12 tribes. By the time this task was completed, however, Joshua was an old man, and he knew he was not much longer for this earth.

In the final chapter of this book, therefore, Joshua calls his people together and gives them his final address. He reminds them of their vocation to choose—and to keep choosing—the Lord. They are to live according to the commandments that make them a unique people. Because they alone follow the way of the Lord, they are not to intermarry with the nations around them. In so many ways Joshua tells the Israelites that they should not turn to the left or the right, but they should follow the straight path which the Lord has set them upon. Above all, they are to worship Yahweh alone, not believing or trusting in any other gods. If they live according to their vocation, God's power will be theirs. The power that brought them into the promised land will sustain them forever. God will always be faithful to them; they need only be faithful to him. God will always be true to his Word; they need only be true to it also. God will always fulfill his promises; they need only fulfill theirs.

Joshua reminds the people of all that God has done for them, beginning with the call of Abraham, the choosing of Isaac and Jacob, and the sending of Moses into Egypt. Yahweh is the God who rescued them from slavery, who found them in the desert, who brought them into the Promised Land. Now he has given them towns they did not build, fields they did not work, and vineyards they did not plant. It has all been gift. It is all grace.

But now they must decide: Are they going to remember Yahweh or forget about him? They must decide: Are they going to serve the Lord or turn to other gods? They must decide: Are they going to trust in God's power or in their own efforts? They cannot have it both ways, and Joshua tells them so.

It is the same with us. The Word of God speaks to us through the book of Joshua, and it says to us that we too, here and now, must make the same decision that the Israelites faced. We too have to choose between God and other gods. We have to choose between his power and our power. We have to choose between his Kingdom and the world.

Either God is God, or not. Either God is everything, or God is, in fact, nothing. Religion has become so much a matter of playing in the in-between, calling God "God" when he is, in fact, not God to us. He is just a religious image that people feel some vague obligation toward because they have been told that he saved them. But they have not experienced his salvation the way the Israelites did.

Once you have experienced that salvation, once you have felt God's power in your life, once you have been touched by his love in your heart, then you know what this book of the Bible is all about. Once you have truly listened to God's Word, once you have heard his promise and seen it fulfilled, then you really know the faithfulness that never fails. Perhaps things do not always work out the way you wish, but they always work out, and they always work out unto good.

In our New Jerusalem Community we have seen this happen again and again, sometimes in surprising and unexpected ways, but we have seen it over and over and over again. And I too, in my own life, can see that the Lord has been so faithful to his promise. Everything I ever asked of the Lord has already been given to me. If I were to die today, I would have to admit that he has already done all that I asked of him. The deepest desires of my boyhood have been fulfilled in overflowing abundance.

This is the same experience the Israelites had when Joshua spoke his last words to them. They know God's faithfulness. They know he has given them all that they ever dreamed of. And so when Joshua asks them for their decision, they choose the Lord. They promise to be faithful to him, just as he has been faithful to them. After Joshua hears this, he is able to die in peace.

And yet we know that it is not that simple. It is never that simple. The next book of the Bible, the Book of Judges, shows why.

Judges

The judges were leaders that the Lord raised up in the midst of Israel to keep the people faithful to their promise. We call them judges, but they were not judges in the modern sense of that term. They were charismatic figures, men with the gift of leadership. They were judges in the sense that they made decisions; that is, they kept making the decision that the Israelites had made when they decided to choose Yahweh over other gods. They kept reminding the people of their decision, reminding them of Yahweh's faithfulness, and helping them to keep choosing the Lord.

In the Book of Judges, we see a single pattern repeated

time and again: The Israelites forget God's love, are oppressed by their enemies, turn back to God and are delivered; then they forget again, are oppressed, repent and are freed again. This pattern emerges for the first time in the second chapter: The people of Joshua's generation have died, and the next generation has no experience of what Yahweh has done for them.

The message is clear: God has no grandchildren. Every generation has to be converted anew. Every person has to experience the love and fidelity of God. And every person has to make the choice for God, to decide to base his or her life on God's Word.

It is not enough to say that your mother is a Christian, that your father is a Catholic. Until you come to that moment in your own life when you choose the God you will serve, you have not been converted. And the reason why the Scriptures do not speak to most Catholics in our own day is, quite simply, that they have never experienced this conversion. Since they have not heard God's Word in their lives, they cannot respond to God's Word in the Bible.

The sixth chapter of Judges begins the story of Gideon. The Israelites had become unfaithful to Yahweh; they had turned to other gods. Then a nearby tribe, the Midianites, started to invade the land. They harrassed the Israelites, destroyed their crops and rustled their cattle. Finally, in their distress, the Israelites recognized their infidelity and turned to the Lord, asking him to save them.

Responding to their plea, Yahweh now sends a message to a young farmer. An angel appears to Gideon and addresses him in words similar to the salutation which we know so well from the New Testament scene of the annunciation: "The Lord is with you, mighty soldier!" Of course Gideon is confused, just as Mary was. He thinks he's just a farm boy. "Forgive me, sir," Gideon answers, "but if Yahweh is with me, why is all this happening to us? Why isn't God working miracles like the ones we're told he used to work in Egypt?" (Judges 6:12-13).

How much like us he sounds! We look at all the evil in the world and say, how can God be with us? How can he be a God of love? How can he be a God of power? It seems that God has deserted us. We do not see that all too often it is we who have deserted God. But he is there, patiently waiting to respond to our plea.

So the Lord, through his angel, tells Gideon, "I will give you the strength you need to rescue Israel from the Midianites. You will defeat them as though they were a lone soldier" (Judges 6:14-16). Then the biblical writer describes a scene in which the angel performs a miracle to show that he had truly come from Yahweh. But what did Gideon really see? Most likely there was no great vision. Probably he came to an awareness of God's call in the same way you and I do. The Lord calls us to something more, to do something that we feel incapable of. Our first impulse is to doubt: We cannot believe it is the Lord who is speaking to us. We doubt we have the strength to do it, and so we cannot believe the call is from the Lord. We easily forget that God is not asking us to do it on our own. The next scene in the story shows this perfectly.

Gideon sends messengers to tell the tribes of Israel that Yahweh is about to deliver them, and so Israel puts together a great army to go out and face the enemy. But the Lord says to Gideon, "You have too many men, if I am to defeat the Midianites for you. With all these soldiers, the Israelites might take the credit and tell me that they are the ones who won the battle. Go out among your men and tell the ones who are timid or afraid to go home" (Judges 7:2-3). So Gideon cuts his army down to a third of its original size, but there are still 10,000 left.

Yahweh sees this and says, "Ten thousand! That's still too many! Are you going to trust me or aren't you?" He wants to show them that they will win not by their might but by his, and so he says to Gideon, "Send the army down to drink at the spring, and I will give them a test." Most of the soldiers keep their weapons in their hands but put their faces in the water to drink. Some of them lay their weapons down and cup the water in their hands to drink it. Then the Lord says, "Okay, I want just those, the ones who put down their weapons, because they trusted me enough. They're all right. Send the others home." So Gideon cuts his army down to 300 men, because the others couldn't trust enough to risk disarmament, even for one moment. They had to protect themselves. They are just like us: We're always fighting our own battles, and as long as that continues, we say to God that we don't need him. That's the whole point of this story.

The time has come to put the Lord's plan into effect. Shortly after midnight, Gideon and his soldiers surround the thousands of Midianites in their camp. And what weapons do they carry with them? Not swords and shields, but trumpets and torches. At a given signal, they uncover their torches and blow their trumpets, shouting, "For Yahweh and Gideon!" The enemy is seized with panic. They begin fighting and killing each other, and after getting thoroughly confused, they flee in all directions! The Israelites are victorious, but it is the Lord who has given them the total victory (Judges 7:1-22).

The lesson here is once again the theme of monotheism: the idea of having one God in your life, only one. But how do you know, practically speaking, who the gods are in your life? Who are you counting on to save you? Logic and reason? Your IRA? The Pentagon? The National Security State? When you're not busy doing something, what do you dream about? What are you hoping for in life? What do you believe will finally make you happy? Whoever it is, or whatever it is, that's your god. That's the god you're bowing before, that's the lord of your life. And if your lord is not Yahweh, then you are letting other gods come before him.

You would think the Israelites would realize this. But no, after this great triumph the people come to Gideon and ask *him* to be their lord. But he refuses: "It is not I who should rule over you, nor my son. Your lord must be Yahweh" (Judges 8:23). As long as Gideon lives, therefore, the people remember Yahweh and worship him. But after Gideon's death, the Israelites once again start turning to other gods, other idols, other baals, as the Bible calls them.

And so the story goes. Other judges come after Gideon. Sometimes the Israelites are faithful to Yahweh; sometimes they are not. But during all this time, they do not have a king. In their form of government, if not always in their lives, they maintain the theocratic ideal that Yahweh is the one true king and lord of Israel. It is a preparation for Jesus' proclamation of the Kingdom, where only God's truth reigns.

In the 13th chapter of the Book of Judges, we come across

another figure with whom most of us are familiar, the hero Samson. This is the kind of Bible story that makes God seem unreal to us, if we don't know how to read it. The story seems to say that Samson's strength was in his hair. Because we know from our own experience that this cannot be true, we start thinking that the Scriptures are not true, and we fail to find the truth within the story.

To understand the lesson of the story, we have to look at it within its Jewish context. Samson's mother dedicated him to God, and as a sign of his being set aside to do the Lord's work, no razor was to ever touch his head. This is called the nazarite vow, and we see evidence of this even today among those orthodox Jews who wear long side locks of hair. Uncut hair was a sign of the nazarite's fidelity to God. So by not cutting his hair Samson remained faithful to his consecration to the Lord. Long hair was a sign of his trust in God.

Because Samson has the strength of God within him, Samson can perform mighty feats. He kills a lion with his bare hands. He kills a thousand Philistines (by this time the Philistines have replaced the Midianites as the enemies of Israel) with the jawbone of a donkey. Nothing can stop him!

There probably was a man like Samsom somewhere back in Israel's history, someone who attributed his amazing strength to God. In the telling and retelling of his story over centuries, his strength grew to gigantic proportions and his deeds became unbelievably awesome. But that's the way it is with oral history. It's the point of the story, not the details, that matters. The point here is this: Samson's strength came from God, and he kept his strength as long as he kept faithful to his vow to leave his hair uncut.

Enter Delilah. We see something of the legendary nature of this story in her name, which means "a female traitor." Samson falls in love with her, and the Philistines promise her a lot of money if she can discover the source of his strength. Time and again she asks him; time and again he fools her and refuses to tell. At last, however, he gives in, and he tells her his secret. The source of his strength is his consecration to the Lord, symbolized by his uncut hair. So Delilah lulls Samson to sleep, and the Philistines come in and cut his hair. Shorn of his power by having trusted in a traitor rather than in God, Samson is chained and thrown in prison by his enemies, who let him out from time to time so they can mock him. But as his hair grows back, his strength returns, and finally he defeats his captors by pulling down the pillars of the palace where they are entertaining themselves at his expense.

The great themes of this story echo throughout this book of the Bible: surrender to God, dedication to God first, and reliance on spiritual power rather than on one's own. These are the secrets that were known to Joshua, to Gideon and to Samson. They were the source of Samson's strength. These ideas that the Scripture writers preserved and established so richly in their inspiring mixture of fact and legend are good news: They proclaim that the secret of life has been revealed to us by the very source of life. In this book we see that good news slowly working its way into human consciousness, accepted and then rejected, believed and then discarded as incredible. For sure, we still have a way to go.

1 and 2 Samuel

Beginning with the books of Samuel, we can see a tension starting to develop between charism and institution, between the freedom of the Spirit and the inertia of society. Israel started out as a people on the move, following the lead of the Lord. During the period of the judges they followed charismatic leaders in times of crisis. But by about the 10th century before Christ, however, they were starting to become a large and settled nation in the land of Palestine. They found themselves needing more structure, more organization, even more bureaucracy to keep themselves together as a people.

Any prayer group has experienced this same sort of tension as it starts to develop into a community. It is so real to all of us who were in New Jerusalem from the very beginning. It was so nice when we were a few people who prayed in a room together! We could go merrily on our way, trusting in the Lord, and everything would work out fine. But then the group got larger. We had to have more meetings; we had to take care of this and that; we needed more organization. At that point it gets very easy to stop trusting in the Lord and to start doing it all yourself.

Having gone through that ourselves, it becomes much easier to be patient and understanding with the Church. For 2,000 years, Catholics have been trying to be the people of God, and there has always been this tension between the charismatic and the institutional dimensions of the Church. Certainly we have been the whore of Babylon, but we have also been the bride of Christ. Surely we have been unfaithful, but in the midst of all that infidelity there has always been a lot of faithfulness. The vision of faith sees the divine in the human, the presence of God in the midst of his people. We develop large social structures to hold it all together, but always the Lord sends us prophets to call us back to the central core of our faith, which is trust and fidelity.

Returning to the Scriptures, we see this tension starting to develop when the people ask the prophet Samuel to institute a monarchy in Israel:

> "Give us a king to rule over us, like the other nations." It displeased Samuel that they should say, "Let us have a king to rule us," so he prayed to Yahweh. But Yahweh said to Samuel, "Obey the voice of the people in all that they say to you, for it is not you they have rejected; they have rejected me from ruling over them....Well then, obey their voice; only, you must warn them solemnly and instruct them in the rights of the king who is to reign over them."
>
> (1 Samuel 8:7-9 JB)

From the very outset it is clear that this new institution is a concession to the weakness of the people: They need to have a visible ruler. Yahweh chooses Saul to be their king, but Samuel admonishes them:

> If you reverence and serve Yahweh and obey his voice and do not disobey his order, and if

both you and the king who rules over you follow
Yahweh your God, all will be well. But if you
do not obey the voice of Yahweh, if you rebel
against his order, his hand will be against you
and against your king. (1 Samuel 12:14-15 JB)

In other words, the Lord through his prophet tells the people:
It is all right to have a king, but don't take him too seriously!
Both the king and the people still have to listen to the Lord and
be open to the Spirit.

The tragedy of the Church is that we often lose this
wisdom. Instead of trusting in the Lord and being led by the
Spirit, we turn the work of the Church over to professionals and
bureaucrats. We see a problem, so we start a program and hire
someone to administer it. We see another problem, so we start
a new program, and then another. Soon we need a department
to coordinate all the programs, and an office to run them from,
and a staff to keep the whole business running smoothly. Pretty
soon the organization takes on a life of its own, and the
institutional bureaucracy rolls on year after year, decade after
decade, whether or not the needs are still there, whether or not
the original programs are still the best way to meet them. We
take our institutions too seriously, and we invest them with
authority which the Lord would not give even to a king that he
himself appointed.

In New Jerusalem, even as large as we have been getting,
we find it very helpful to spend a long while listening to the
Lord before making an important community decision.
Sometimes we, like many others in Christian ministry, find
ourselves moving on our own steam, going off in different
directions, trying to take care of problems inside and outside of
the community without any unifying sense of the Spirit's
guidance. We start to feel tensions between groups,
disagreements about priorities, even mistrust of one another.
At times like that—or, better yet, *before* such times develop—we
come together for a meeting. We come to meet with each other,
certainly, but first of all we come to meet with the Lord. We
spend the first hour opening our hearts to him, letting go of
ourselves and letting God be our Lord. During that time of

prayer, the Lord softens a heart here, enlightens a mind there, brings one to humility, gives another courage. After that meeting in the Spirit, we can usually take care of in a half hour what might otherwise take hours of wrangling and contention to resolve.

How different that is from the usual parish council, school board or diocesan committee meeting! People come in and zip through a Hail Mary, and then follow with two hours of grueling, sometimes frustrating, work. We act as though it's all up to us, as though our efforts can renew the Church, as though our decisions can change the hearts of people. Willfulness remains unchecked.

Yet the Scriptures tell us plainly that it is only God who saves. God alone can bring salvation, even from the difficulties that we have to deal with day by day. If we as Christian ministers allow ourselves to be truly and deeply people of prayer, especially when we come together for our work, we can experience much more power in our lives and we can see much more fruit coming from our labors.

As it is, however, we often take ourselves too seriously, believing in ourselves rather than in the Lord. And that's exactly what Saul does. Not being content to just be king, he wants to be the master of it all; he wants to play God. So the Lord rejects Saul's kingship, not because he didn't try hard, but because he did not stay in touch with God. He lost the spirit with which he had been anointed.

So Samuel goes out to find another king. (By now he is an old man. You can just see him wishing that this king will be the right one so he can die in peace!) The Lord sends him to Bethlehem to find a man named Jesse and to anoint one of his sons. One by one Jesse brings out his sons to meet the prophet, beginning with the eldest. They're all big, strong, handsome lads, but Yahweh has told Samuel, "Pay no attention to their face or height. God does not see as man sees. Man judges by appearances, but I look into the heart" (1 Samuel 16:7). So one by one Samuel passes them all up. "Is this all of them?" the prophet asks Jesse. It turns out there is one more son. He's a little short guy out in the field taking care of the sheep. Samuel says, "I want to see him. Bring him in." The youngest son, of

course, is David, and as soon as Samuel sees him Yahweh says,
"This is the one!" So right there on the spot Samuel anoints
David to be king over all the people.

This is another example of how the Lord's choice is so
often different from our own. This is another of the great themes
running all through the Scriptures. God chooses Abraham, a
nobody, and makes him a somebody. God chooses Jacob over
Esau, even though Esau is the elder son and Jacob is a shifty
character. God even chooses Saul out of Benjamin, the smallest
and weakest tribe in Israel. Now God chooses David, the
youngest and the least experienced son of an ordinary father,
to be king over the nation. If we listen to the Lord, the way the
prophet Samuel did, how often our decisions might be different!
The last might be first and the first might be last.

The Lord indeed is with David. That's the lesson to be
learned from the story about David's fight with Goliath in
chapter 17. It is the same theme found in the story about the
walls of Jericho, only this time the obstacle is a man who is built
like a wall. As with Samson, there is probably a grain of historical
truth to the description of this Philistine giant, but by the time
the story got written down Goliath had grown to be 10 feet tall!
The point of the story, however, is simple. It's the story of a
boy facing a man. It's the story of a shepherd fighting a soldier.
It's the story of a person facing impossible odds. And it's the
story of how God evens up the odds, if we are in union with
the Center, in love with the Lord.

As David goes out to meet Goliath, he trusts in the Lord.
The frightened and weary Saul (who does not know yet about
David's anointing) wants to dress him in heavy armor, but David
doesn't need that. Yahweh will be his armor. Saul wants to give
him big weapons, but David refuses. Instead, David picks up a
stone for his slingshot and with God's help he uses a child's toy
to do a man's work. You'll notice that God doesn't strike Goliath
down with lightning or something. God needs us to do his work.
Here we see the beginning of the theme of incarnation, which
does not get fully developed until the New Testament. But even
at this point in the Scriptures we are seeing how God can act
through us if we step out in faith. Because David knew his power
came from God, and because he did it for the glory of the Lord,

David was able to do the impossible. It's the same with us.

David was always a man who gloried in the Lord. He loved the Lord with all his heart. Like kids today with their guitars, David played his harp and sang his songs, but many of them he sang to God. Many of the psalms in the Bible are said to have been written by him. David even danced before the Lord. When he was king, he danced around the ark of the covenant in public. His wife was embarrassed, but he was not afraid to be a child before the Lord, even at the risk of looking foolish. Think of that the next time you attend a solemn liturgy! Why can't our bishops and pastors be more like David? Why can't *we* be more like him?

Yet David was not perfect, either. Later in his life he fell in love with Bathsheba, the beautiful wife of one of his generals. So that he could have her for himself, he sent her husband into a battle where he was sure to get killed. Yahweh sent the prophet Nathan to accuse David of his sin, and unlike so many others in power, David accepted the rebuke. He realized he had been untrue to himself and unfaithful to God, and he expressed his repentance in a poem that we now call Psalm 51.

This is why David is such a model for the Church right now. In a period of change, he learned by trial and error, and he was able to admit his mistakes. As king he represents the institutional element in the Church, its power and authority; but he also listens to the charismatic element, represented by the prophet. During this period, unlike any other in the history of Israel, we see the working together of institution and charism to build up the people of God. King and prophet listen to each other, respect each other and learn from each other. In that coming together there is power, the kind of power that is available when no one relies on self alone and everyone relies on the Lord and seeks the common truth.

In the Second Book of Samuel we see another great theme emerge: grace. We have already see examples of this, for grace means gift, and everything the Israelites accomplished thus far has been a gift from God. But in 2 Samuel we discover a shining example of this.

In chapter 7 David has achieved final victory over the Philistines, he has set up his capital in Jerusalem, and he has built himself a fine home there.* The ark of the covenant, however, is still kept in a large tent, as it was in the days when the Israelites were a nomadic people. So David goes to the prophet Nathan and says, "Look, I am living in a house of cedar while the ark of God remains in a tent" (2 Samuel 7:2). David is saying, in other words, that he wants to build a house for God, a temple. That very night, however, the Lord lets the prophet know his reply to the king's request:

> Why do you want to build me a house? I have never lived in a temple! From the time I brought the Israelites out of Egypt until today, my home has been a tent....I took you from being a shepherd in the pasture and made you the leader of my people Israel. I went with you on all your expeditions, and I cut down your enemies. Now I will make you as famous as the greatest men on earth. I will provide a homeland for my people Israel,...and I will give them rest from the attacks of their enemies. Moreover, I will make you a house. And when your days are over and you lay to rest with your forefathers, I will preserve your offspring and make his kingdom secure. (2 Samuel 7:5-12)

What are we to make of this? What is the Lord saying here? He is saying, "It's very nice of you to offer to build me a house, but I don't need it! Instead, I will make *you* a house." People always want to do something for God. And what does God want? He wants to do something for them!

The biblical message is the other side of the catechism answer which said that we are made to know, love and serve God. The biblical message is that God made us so he could know us and love us and serve us. That's the central meaning of grace: God giving us himself, his love and his help. It is a perfect and whole experience of being loved. It is more than we could ever

---

* The Roman name for the area, Palestine, means "land of the Philistines."

ask, and so God does not wait for us to ask it. He gives us this life freely and spontaneously, generously and continuously. And that's why living in God's grace is living in power. All we have to do is be open to it, receive it, trust it and treasure it.

People are always trying to build temples and churches for God. And what is God trying to do? He is trying to build us into a temple, a living temple, a temple of the Holy Spirit, as St. Paul says (1 Corinthians 3:16-17). The people of God is the house of God, the place where God dwells on earth. Likewise, the house of David is not the building he lives in but the family of David, the decendants of David who continue in his tradition of trusting and serving the Lord, willingly and even joyfully. So grace builds up the house of David, the people of God, the temple of the Holy Spirit, the body of Christ. The creation of the Church is a gift of grace, and we see it starting even here, thousands of years ago.

During David's time, then, we begin to see the reversal of that pattern which we saw earlier. During the time of the judges, Israel would forget Yahweh's love for them, be oppressed, repent and be delivered. Now Israel starts seeing that Yahweh delivers them even before they repent. They are beginning to see the unconditional love of God. They are coming to see that there is nothing they can do to merit salvation and deliverance. God delivers and redeems simply because that is who God is. God is the liberator; God is the one who frees. God is the lover, always the initiator. And we can never be "worthy."

Again, this is the theme of grace. When people turn from the Lord and sin, they experience harmful consequences because evil by its very nature leads to evil. And so they repent, they turn themselves around and start doing good. But here Israel is beginning to see that God loves them, not because they repent, but even before they repent. In fact, it is the awareness of God's unfailing love which leads to true repentance, to a true change of heart. Authentic repentance always comes from the experiences that God has first loved us, and in that we find the power to love in return. Meister Eckhart put it this way centuries later: "The eyes by which we look back at God are the very same eyes by which God first looked at us."

1 and 2 Kings

As we move forward into the books of 1 and 2 Kings, we see that the delicate balance between charism and institution begins to waver. David's son is Solomon, who is renowned for his wisdom. The Book of Proverbs is attributed to him, as well as much of the other wisdom literature in the Bible, just as the psalms are attributed to David. During the reign of Solomon the kingdom of Israel really gets organized. He establishes trade with Israel's neighbors; he gets into mining, shipping and manufacturing; he builds up the army, and he builds a great temple in Jerusalem for the glory of God.

As long as Solomon is alive, all seems to go well, but institutionalization is starting to take over. The triumphalism of the kingly is beginning to outweigh the realism of the prophetic. Everything is becoming task-oriented. The Israelites begin to see themselves as accomplishing something, doing something by their own power instead of by God's power. It's all building and doing, building and doing. Even the temple liturgy becomes magnificent and spectacular. We understand how that happens, because we have seen it happen in the Church.

All the while, the delicate balance is being undone. Most of this building and trading is going on in the south, and money is pouring into Jerusalem. But the people in the north are burdened with taxes. Their young men are forced into the army and into construction work. They begin to feel alienated from the temple worship. They begin to feel the injustice of the imbalance.

And so, when Solomon dies, the tribes of the north revolt against the triumphalism of the south, and the country is divided. The 10 northern tribes establish themselves as the political kingdom of Israel, with their own king and their own temple. The two southern tribes become the political kingdom of Judah. Rampant institutionalism takes its toll. Solomon ruins the whole nation with his military budget and his spiritual blindness.

We have seen this pattern in the Church's history as well.

In the Middle Ages, Christendom was ruled from "the south," by Rome. As time went on, however, triumphalism in the south became rampant. Great cathedrals and basilicas were built (including the magnificent St. Peter's), the popes and bishops lived in palaces, and liturgies were spectacular. Somehow in all this institutionalism the Spirit was lost, the image of Christ was obscured. So the Christians in "the north" (Germany) revolted, trying to reform the Church. And in seeking to regain the Spirit, they broke away from the institution. Protestantism began.

There was a time when we Catholics viewed the Protestant reformation as all bad, but it was the wisdom of the Second Vatican Council to see that the picture was not black and white. The Council rediscovered the wisdom of the Scriptures, and the Scriptures tell us that the northern tribes were not all bad and the southern tribes were not all good. The northern tribes "left the Church," as it were, and Judah still had the original institutions, but it had lost the Spirit, that charismatic spirit of God which alone breathes life into institutions.

Separated from their southern brothers and sisters, the northern tribes also lost the spirit of Yahweh. They gave in to their own institutionalism and triumphalism. Many Protestants will tell you that the same thing happened to their own churches. This is something we can learn from Christian history, and we can get some insight into our own history by meditating on biblical history.

Even at the height of institutionalization (or perhaps because of it), the charismatic spirit of God tries to break through to restore the balance. We can see this in our own century, in those prophetic voices which spoke in the Church before the calling of the Second Vatican Council.

During the biblical period of the divided kingdom, that voice was heard through the prophet Elijah. In the 19th chapter of 1 Kings, Yahweh leads him out into the Sinai desert, through which the Israelites had passed so many years before, out to the mountain where God had made the covenant with them and given the commandments. There Elijah gets in touch with the heart of their tradition, God's loving initiative and their trusting response. And then he returns to preach to the people.

He calls the people to return to their roots, to return to

the covenant. He warns them that if they do not, if they try to preserve their petty kingdoms by their own power, they will be destroyed by their enemies. His message to them is not just religious; it has social and political implications, as all the prophets' messages do.

After Elijah comes Elisha, as described in 2 Kings. His prophetic message is the same: Return to the Lord, return to the covenant. Do not put your trust in false gods and foreign alliances. It is Yahweh who will save you, not your own strength and your own cleverness. But the people do not listen; nor do the kings listen.

Eventually, despite Elijah and despite Elisha, both kingdoms remain unfaithful to the covenant. They forget the love of God. They forget that Yahweh freed them from slavery. They forget that Yahweh led them through the desert. They forget that it is God who gave them life. And so Israel, the northern kingdom, falls to the Assyrians in 721 B.C. These 10 tribes are deported and scattered through the Middle East. We never hear from them again. They are sometimes called the lost tribes of Israel.

Frightened, the king of the southern kingdom initiates a reform, destroying idols and restoring the worship of Yahweh in the temple. But the reform is only halfhearted. In 587, Judah falls to the Babylonians. Jerusalem is captured, and the temple is destroyed.

What were the people to make of this? Had Yahweh gone back on his promise? Had he stopped loving them? The people of Judah were carried off into exile for 60 years, and many of them did not return from that Babylonian captivity. Those who did, returned to Judah (or Judaea, as it was called later on by the Romans), which is why their descendents today are called the Jews. They were all that was left of the original 12 tribes of Israel.

In time, the Jews also resettled the northern territory, now called Galilee, which is where Jesus grew up and spent the greater portion of his ministry. Between Judaea and Galilee there was an area called Samaria, inhabited by non-Jews whose religious traditions were a mixture of Israelite and pagan customs. The Samaritans saw themselves as descendants of the old northern kingdom, but to the Jews they were half-breeds and heretics, which is why the Jews in Jesus' day looked down on them.

But that's far off yet, five centuries in the future. At this point the Jews are in exile, trying to fathom the ways of God, trying to understand what happened to them. Eventually, they come to realize what we can see so clearly now, looking back on their history. The divided kingdom, the downfall and the exile were caused by infidelity to their covenant with Yahweh. The king and the kingdom had stopped being servants of God and had become self-serving instead. They had become an end in themselves.

Nothing in this world is an end in itself, not even the Church. Only God is an end; everything else is a means, a means to that end. Only God saves; nothing else can save us. Not the law, not the Bible, not the Pope, not the sacraments, not even the Church. The Church is God's free gift to us, through which we come to hear his Word and allow him to save us. When we make means into ends, we forget that. We think we are putting God first, but really we are putting ourselves first.

Jesus understood this perfectly. If the Church is the *new* Israel, as we sometimes say, we have to remember that Jesus grew up in the *old* Israel, the original people of God. Yet Jesus never put Israel first; he put God first. He preached about Yahweh, and the Father's love, and fidelity to that love. He did not preach about Israel. Nevertheless, Jesus did not put Israel down; he loved Israel. In the same way we should not put the Church first. We should "seek first the kingdom and God's justice," but we should not fight the Church unless it makes itself an idol. We should love the Church. God loves the Church today, just as he loved Israel.

If we love the Church, however, we must love it as it is, for that is how God loves it. We cannot love it as it was 50 years ago; that Church is gone. We cannot love it as it will be 50 years from now; that Church has not arrived yet. The only Church that exists is the Church today, and the only real love for the Church is for the people who are in it now.

This is not to say we must accept the institution blindly. That's the mistake Israel made. We must not think our institutions—or our laws, our customs, our creeds, or even our sacraments—are ends in themselves. Many times, when people do or say things differently from the way we do, we put them down. The Jews despised the Samaritans, but the Lord said even the Samaritans are good.

The truth that the Scriptures reveal to us is not an institution. Scriptural truth is a person, and a relationship with a person. It is a relationship of love that we enter into not only with the divine person but with every person that we meet. In that relationship of love, truth happens. It is the truth about God, and the truth about ourselves. In that relationship of love, we are saved from clinging to our institutions and everything that is not God. In that truth we are set free.

CHAPTER FOUR

The Prophets:
Radical Traditionalists

Passionate, imaginative, and at times enigmatic, the prophetic literature in the Bible speaks to us today as forcefully as it did in ancient times. We have only to let the prophetic Word penetrate our hearts and subvert our systems of security, as it did Israel's.

What It Means to Be a Prophet

Listen to the prophet Jeremiah describing the power of God's Word when it came to him:

> You deceived me, Yahweh, and I was seduced.
> You were too strong for me, and you
> overpowered me. Now I am the laughingstock
> of the city, the butt of everybody's joke.
> Whenever I speak what you tell me, I have to
> announce violence and destruction! The word
> of the Lord has brought me nothing but insult
> and derision.
>
> I tell myself not to think about him; I try
> not to speak his name. But then the word feels
> like a fire in my heart, like a burning coal in my
> bones. I get tired of trying to hold it in. I can't
> bear it any longer! (Jeremiah 20:7-9)

This description is dramatic, to be sure. Not every prophet feels he has to fight what God is telling him to say. And yet this passage makes a point. In every age God sends prophets, but every age rejects them because the Word of God is a two-edged sword. Sometimes it is a comforting word, but more often it is a disquieting word.

The prophets stand in our midst and tell it like it is, speaking the disturbing word that people don't want to hear. If you find that the Word of God has not placed a demand on you, or challenged your life, you have not yet heard it. If it has not called you to death, to lay down your life, to forget about yourself, you have not yet heard it. If it has not called you where you do not want to go, you have not yet heard the voice of the prophets nor the Word that speaks through them.

Jesus knew well what being a prophet meant. He knew that most of the prophets had been rejected, even put to death, by the very people they tried to serve. For the most part the prophets were sent to speak to religious people, synagogue-going people, churchgoers just like us. But these "good" people were too comfortable in their religiousness to listen to the prophets' uncomfortable word.

For the prophet is not so much one who sees into the future as one who sees clearly in the present. He is not so much a man of foresight as a man of insight. Such a person right now, in the present, listens to the Lord and speaks the word he or she hears. The prophet hears what is real, and he speaks it to the world. But the world too often does not want to see reality, and so it turns a deaf ear on the prophet.

Prophets are seldom establishment people. They often have to confront institutional theology, which can make the status quo seem to have divine approval. Established traditions often wield a power they do not deserve. If they do not serve the purpose of God, they serve other masters. If traditions are not constantly called into question, they become idols. The greatest of these idols are institutions, and the most potentially dangerous is the one we call the Church.

Prophets in Israel often came into conflict with the established leaders of their day, guarding their established traditions. Jesus himself, the last and greatest of the prophets of Israel, spoke his strongest words against the priests and scribes of the temple, and he was condemned to death by the leaders of religion. Prophets in our own day, men and women both, often come into conflict with the clergy and the hierarchy. It's nice when this does not happen, but it often does.

The most important theme in all the prophets' messages is that of faithfulness: the faithfulness of God and the faithfulness of the people. The prophets were the social conscience of Israel, just as prophets in our own day are people of great conscience. We like to believe that what we are doing is in line with what God wants us to do, but sometimes we take off along in our own direction unaware that it is no longer God's direction. We idolize our own direction, enshrining it in laws and regulations, surrounding it with a halo of respectability. We say this is what God wants, but really it is what we want. Pretty soon a prophet comes along who speaks for God, the way Isaiah did: "These people say that they are mine, but it is only lip service. Their hearts are far from me, and their religion is just a human institution" (Isaiah 29:13). The prophet's message pricks the conscience and calls us back to truth.

The basis of that appeal to conscience is the other side of the prophetic message: God's faithfulness to us. To communicate this in a special way, God once told the prophet Hosea to take back his unfaithful wife, Gomer. Hosea did that; but not long after, Gomer ran off with another man. The Lord said take her back again, and Hosea dutifully obeyed. But pretty soon his wife left him to have another affair. This happened again and again, and after a while Hosea was getting pretty fed up with it all. He didn't want to take her back, even though the Lord was telling him to keep loving her.

Then the prophet had an insight into what was going on. Israel had been unfaithful to Yahweh, prostituting herself before other gods; but Yahweh's love kept reaching out to Israel, drawing her back to himself. God was faithful, even though the people were not. And so the Lord was asking this man of God to do what God was doing, so that the people could see what the love of God was really like. The Lord was patiently, faithfully waiting for the day when Israel would return at last to him: "When that day comes, she will call me, 'My husband.' ...I will love her even though she feels unloved. I will say to her, 'You are my people,' and she will answer, 'You are my God'" (Hosea 2:16, 23).

The story of Hosea illustrates how prophetic insight often works. First of all, it's a matter of hindsight. Prophets look into the past and see what God has done in history. They perceive the pattern of God's creative love, his call to trust in him, and the unexpected life he gives to those who put their faith in him and him alone. They perceive this pattern in the Exodus from Egypt, in the conquest of Canaan, in the founding of the Davidic kingdom. The pattern is also the pattern of salvation: always God loving, always God calling, always God giving new life. By reflecting on the past, the prophets also see that when people broke away from that pattern, when they did not believe in God's love or respond to God's call, they walked into death instead of life; they experienced injustice, oppression and destruction.

Second, the prophets turn their vision to the present. They look into the present situation to see which pattern can be detected in the world around them: Is it the pattern of salvation, which leads to life, or is it the pattern of sin, which leads to death? If their prophetic insight tells them that it is the latter, they proclaim: "This is not the way of God! You're going in the wrong direction!"

Third, and finally, prophetic insight becomes foresight of a sort. The prophet sees what is coming if people do not live according to the divine pattern but choose some other pattern of their own. They cannot tell the future, but they can tell the future will be bad unless the people change their ways. They cannot see what will happen later on, but they can see that right now things are going in a direction which can only lead to ruin. The prophet Jeremiah, as we have seen, felt the burden of his insight into the impending destruction of Jerusalem.

So the prophets reflect on the past, speak to the present and point to the future. In speaking to the present, though, they often find themselves saying things that people do not want to hear. What Jeremiah felt compelled to say, for example, sounded unpatriotic, unrealistic, and not in the national self-interest of Judah. But true prophets are always saying things like that. They are always against nationalism and the kinds of things that lead to it. Even though Christians for centuries have believed that nationalism is a good thing, it goes directly against the prophetic message. We could even say that it is unscriptural. But who wants to hear that today? People did not want to listen to it in biblical times, either.

And yet the prophets were all optimists. They were always optimistic because they had seen the redemptive pattern of the Lord. They saw God's love breaking through again and again, overcoming human doubt and resistance, bringing salvation and new life. They saw it happen, and they believed in it. Even though they shouted what amounts to, "Shape up! Listen to the Lord!," they carried in their heart the confidence that God would prevail even if the people didn't shape up and didn't listen. Without that confidence they would not have been prophets. They knew for sure that the Word was true, and that the truth would win in the end.

We have to admit, though, that the prophets were sometimes pessimistic optimists! They were sometimes pessimistic about the immediate future, if the people refused to change, refused to convert back to God. And they were always pessimistic about the plans that people had to save themselves. But they also saw clearly that God alone is God. Their prophetic insight told them that somehow, despite all the resistance, despite all the foolishness, despite all the destruction, the Lord was going to win.

A Closer Look at Some of the Prophets

The prophets who have books named after them in the Bible are called the "writing prophets." Some of these books or portions of them were written by the prophets themselves. Others were undoubtedly written by scribes who collected what a prophet said and did, and then edited these collections into their present form. The writing prophets appeared fairly late in Israel's history, however, toward the end of the divided kingdom.

Before the rise of the writing prophets, there were other

prophetic figures in Israel's history, and these are called "the nonwriting prophets." They appear in the books of 1 and 2 Samuel, 1 and 2 Kings, and 1 and 2 Chronicles. Samuel, Nathan, Elijah and Elisha are the greatest of the nonwriting prophets. (Moses does not fit neatly into either category. He was clearly a prophetic figure, but most of the writings attributed to him are not prophetic in character.)

The earliest of the writing prophets was Amos. He lived in the eighth century B.C., when the two kingdoms were still in existence. Amos prophesied in the northern kingdom, as did Hosea, the prophet of God's unrelenting love for the adulterous Israel. The great theme of Amos's prophesy was social justice. He cried out for God on behalf of the poor and oppressed in Israel, against the rich and the powerful:

> Listen to this, you who rob the poor and trample
> on the needy! You cannot wait for the sabbath
> to end and the religious holidays to be over, so
> you can go out and start cheating again, using
> your dishonest scales and measurements. You
> keep the poor in misery by giving them low
> wages and charging them high prices. The Lord
> has sworn that he will not forget your deeds!
> (Amos 8:4-7)

For Amos and the whole biblical tradition, the cause of poverty is simply the oppression and greed of the wealthy—or perhaps sickness and disaster. They never blamed it on laziness or lack of talent. They never blamed the victim as we do today.

Living around the same time, the prophet Micah proclaimed much the same message to the southern kingdom of Judah. He witnessed the destruction of the northern kingdom, and his sympathetic insight foresaw that the same would happen in the south:

> Listen, you rulers of the house of Israel and
> Jacob! You are supposed to know right from
> wrong, yet you hate to do good and love to do
> evil. You tear the skin off my people and strip

them to the bone....
        You hate justice and love unfairness. You
commit murder and fill Jerusalem with crime.
Your judges take bribes, your priests teach only
for money, and your false prophets are no better
than fortune-tellers. You think nothing will
happen to you, saying, "The Lord is with us.
God is on our side." Yet because of you
Jerusalem will be reduced to rubble, the temple
hill will be overgrown with brush, and the city
will be plowed up like a field. (Micah 3:1-3, 9-12)

        In the prophets' words, God is always on the side of the
poor. Today we have come to recognize this essential perspective
again and we rightly speak of "the preferential option for the
poor." God has bias toward the bottom; and the great saints,
like Francis of Assisi and Vincent de Paul and Mother Teresa,
have always shared the same bias.
        The books of Hosea, Amos and Micah are quite short.
The Book of Isaiah, on the other hand, is the longest of the
prophetic works. Modern scholars agree that it was composed
in three different periods by at least three different authors and
later joined into one book. The first part, or First Isaiah (chapters
1 to 39), dates from the eighth century, the period we have just
been discussing. Second Isaiah (chapters 40 to 55) was composed
during the Babylonian exile, perhaps by a woman. And Third
Isaiah (chapters 56 to 66) was composed after the exile. If you
read Isaiah with this in mind, you can see that the authors were
addressing different situations and recounting what the Lord,
through his prophets, was trying to tell the people as their
situation changed.
        The initial Isaiah is the prophet after whom the entire
book is named. Like Micah, he lived in Judah, and he foresaw
the downfall of the southern kingdom because the rulers and
the people had forsaken the ways of the Lord. Again we see
God's judgment on wealth and injustice:

Woe to those who drink from dawn till way after
dark, their heads aglow with wine! They make

69

sure they have lovely music and only the best
wine for their drinking bouts. But they forget
about the Lord and all he did for them. Because
they do not see this, my people will be driven
into exile. The rich and famous will face
starvation, and the common folk will be dying
for a drink of water. (Isaiah 5:11-13)

Zephaniah, Habakkuk and Nahum lived in the middle of
the seventh century, long after the fall of the northern kingdom,
but about a generation before the downfall of the south. Their
prophetic insight told them that the end was approaching, their
securities would not be security and their comforts would offer
them no comfort:

The great day of Yahweh is near, and it is coming
swiftly. Terrible sounds will fill the air, and even
the brave will weep bitterly....
    When the day comes, Jerusalem will be
searched by torchlight, and those who wallow
in the filth of sin will be dragged out and
punished. Those who believe Yahweh can
neither hurt nor help them will see their
prosperity plundered and their homes
ransacked. (Zephaniah 1:14, 12-13)

Nevertheless, the prophets did not give up hope that the
Israelites would once again be "anawim," unpretentious people
who can still hear God and trust in love. They continued to call
the people to repentence:

Look to Yahweh, you who are humble [anawim]
and obey his commands. See yourself for what
you are, and do what is right. You may yet find
shelter on that day of Yahweh's anger.
                            (Zephaniah 2:3)

Jeremiah began his prophetic career just before the
downfall of Jerusalem, and he lived to see the people taken into

exile. In many ways he comes across as the most human of the prophets because his book gives us many biographical details about him. As we saw at the opening of this chapter, he cries out to the Lord, complaining: "Yahweh, you led me into this! I never wanted to be here! I don't want to speak your word. And yet, when I don't, it burns within me" (Jeremiah 20:7,9). It's that two-edged sword again! He cannot run away from God, and yet when he preaches the Word of God, people hate him. "Damn the day I was born!" he wails. "Curse the day my mother brought me into the world!" (Jeremiah 20:14). His anguish almost gets the better of him, but it does not rock his faithfulness to God's call to speak the Word that thunders within him.

He rails against the temple and against those who have made it into an idol, thinking it will protect them:

> The Lord of hosts, the God of Israel, says this:
> "Change your evil ways, amend your lives, and
> I will let you remain in the land." Do not be
> fooled by hymns that sing, "This is the house
> of God, the temple of the Lord." (Jeremiah 7:3-4)

The people think that just because they are Jews, God will save them. They think that just because they have the temple, they are safe. But the temple cannot save them, and in the end, it does not.

In the New Testament, Jesus prophesied again against the temple. The rebuilt temple had again become an idol, a substitute for the true temple which is a body in which God's spirit dwells. This spirit dwelt in Christ and it dwelt in the body of those who were filled with the Holy Spirit in a community of faith and power. The temple God was trying to build was not one made of stone. The Church God is building today is not one made of bricks and mortar.

It's so easy to lose sight of this even in a community like ours, New Jerusalem. One time we were fixing up a building, trying to get it looking nice for a retreat the coming weekend. I was driving everybody hard, giving orders left and right, when one of the kids spilled a can of paint. I yelled at him, but then a young man came and said to me, "Father, all the work doesn't matter. You know that. The reason we're here is to love one another." I had to swallow my pride and realize it was something I had preached in a sermon, but now he was teaching it to me. I was putting my trust in the work of human hands, rather than in the Lord and in what his spirit does among us. It's easy to get lost in building churches and schools and monasteries and retreat houses, and to think that by doing that we are building God's temple on earth. But the temple where God's spirit dwells is the temple that the Lord builds—a community of people who love one another and trust in him.

Just as Jeremiah warned, the temple did not save the people. It lasted almost four hundred years, but it did not last forever. It was destroyed in 587 B.C. There is only one temple that lasts forever, one place where there is eternal life, but it is not a temple made of stones. It is a community of faith, always new, ever changing, assembled wherever two or three are gathered in God's name. God was teaching the Israelites, and slowly they were learning. Oh, how slowly we learn! How long it takes us to learn that lesson, and how often we forget it! It's a hard lesson to learn. The Israelites, the Jews, our forebears in the faith, were learning it the hard way, as often we must also.

Up till this point the prophets had emphasized the people's faith, or rather their lack of it. They had been continually calling the people and their rulers back to the faithfulness they had promised to God. Now, amidst the ruins of their infidelity, the prophetic message changed. They emphasized the faithfulness of God. Before, this had been an intermittent theme. During the exile, however, it became the central theme: God is ever faithful. He is with you even now in exile. You thought you lost a lot, but he will give you even more in the future. His mercy is eternal; his generosity is limitless.

Second Isaiah was written by an unnamed prophet, perhaps a woman disciple of the first Isaiah. Chapters 40 to 55, written during the Babylonian exile, are sometimes called the Book of the Consolation of Israel. It begins,

"Console my people, console them"
says your God.
Speak to the heart of Jerusalem

and call to her
that her time of service is ended,
that her sin is atoned for,
that she has received from the hand of Yahweh
double punishment for all her crimes.

(Isaiah 40:1-2 JB)

The Israelites always perceived everything as coming
from God, even punishment. But the time for punishment was
over now. Before, the people's sin had been pride and
self-reliance; now their sin was despair, another way of not
trusting in the Lord. But God always wants to save his people
from sin, and so he has his prophet say to them:

How can you say, Jacob,
how can you insist, Israel,
"My destiny is hidden from Yahweh,
my rights are ignored by my God"?
Did you not know?
Had you not heard?

Yahweh is an everlasting God,
he created the boundaries of the earth.
He does not grow tired or weary,
his understanding is beyond fathoming.
He gives strength to the wearied,
he strengthens the powerless.
You men may grow tired and weary,
youths may stumble,
but those who hope in Yahweh renew
    their strength,
they put out wings like eagles.
They run and do not grow weary,
walk and never tire. (Isaiah 40:27-41 JB)

So Israel learns. The prophet sees the people becoming
disciples again, servants of God rather than of themselves. Four
beautiful servant songs envision the new Israel that will someday
be:

Each morning he wakes me to hear,
to listen like a disciple.
The Lord Yahweh has opened my ear.

For my part, I made no resistance,
neither did I turn away.
I offered my back to those who struck me,
my cheek to those who tore at my beard;
I did not cover my face
against insult and spittle. (Isaiah 50:4-6 JB)

Centuries later, Christians would see in these songs of
the suffering servant a prefiguration of the suffering Jesus.
Christ was and is the new Israel, and so the words of the prophet
could be rightly applied to him. In the passion of Jesus the words
of the prophet were ultimately fulfilled, which is why these
passages from Isaiah are used every year in the liturgy of Holy
Week.

Gradually, therefore, the prophets directed the hope of
Israel toward the future.

Ezekiel lived through the destruction of Jerusalem and
went with his people into captivity. His prophetic ministry
spanned both periods. In the period before the downfall he
sounded like Jeremiah, calling the people to conversion. But
after their repentence he spoke in a new way to them, giving
them a vision of hope. His prophetic insight saw that there
would be a new Jerusalem, and a new covenant. He heard the
Lord speaking through him:

I shall bring you back from exile, gathering you
together from all the foreign countries, and lead
you home to your own land. Then I shall pour
clean water over you, and all your impurity, all
your idol worship, will be washed away. I shall
give you a new heart, and put a new spirit within
you. I shall take out your heart of stone and give
you in its place a truly human heart. I shall pour
my spirit into you, so that you keep my
commandments and do the things I have told
you. (Ezekiel 36:24-27)

In chapter 16 of Ezekiel there is a long allegorical story of Israel—much too long to be quoted here—which is a beautiful summary of the whole history that we have seen up till now, including a vision of the future which the prophet sees for the people. Paraphrased and shortened somewhat, it goes like this:

You were born in the land of Canaan; your mother and father were idol worshipers. On the day of your birth, no one cared for you, no one washed you or wrapped you in a warm blanket. You were dumped out in a field and left to die, unloved and unwanted.

Then I came by and saw you struggling to live. I picked you up and washed off your blood, and found someone to care for you. You grew into womanhood, straight and tall, lovely and slender. Later I came that way again and saw your beauty. I gave you my cloak, and made a covenant with you, and vowed to marry you. I brought you gifts—silver and gold, silks and linens, jewels and perfumes—and you looked like a queen.

But you became infatuated with your beauty. You loved the gifts I gave you, instead of me. You ran after other men, and took them into your home, and slept with them like a prostitute. You gave my gifts to others, you gave them your soul. Soon there was no place for me in your heart.

So I left. I left you to the mercy of your so-called friends. I left you to their devices, unprotected by my strength. Then they showed themselves for what they really were, rapists every one of them. They robbed you of your finery, they beat your naked body for their own pleasure, and when they were done with you, they ransacked your house and burned it to the ground.

And yet, when all is said and done, I will

treat you as you deserve, though not as others
may think you deserve. You made a covenant
with me in the days of your youth, and I will
remember it. Despite what you have done, I will
be kind to you again. I will honor the vow we
made to each other, and make a new covenant
with you. I shall love you once again, and you
will learn that I am God.

God's love never fails. And his love is forgiveness. God
lets go of the past more quickly than we do. Grace is amazing,
transforming, enriching. He gave life to Israel when she was
dying in slavery. She became beautiful not on her own, but
because God loved her. God gave her gifts, another word for
grace, and love made her even more beautiful. And yet she did
not recognize it, just as we so often don't. She did not thank
him, just as we don't. She did not love him, just as we don't.
The history of Israel is our own story: The Word speaks the truth
of our own lives, both our present and our future. Our past is
as it was; we cannot change that. But our future is with the
Lord, and with his graciousness, if we will just allow forgiveness
and newness to break through.

Ezekiel spoke the Word that came to him in terms of
conversion and a new covenant. He also saw the restoration of
Israel in the image of a new city, a new Jerusalem from which
God's glory would shine out over all the earth. This vision of a
new Jerusalem was developed further by the prophets of the
postexilic period: Zechariah, Obadiah, Joel, Haggai and Third
Isaiah. It is a prophetic vision which appears again in the New
Testament, in the Book of Revelation. Speaking to the old city,
as it were, the desolated Jerusalem, the prophet says:

Lift up your eyes and look round:
all are assembling and coming toward you,
your sons from far away,
and your daughters being tenderly carried.

At this sight you will go radiant,
your heart throbbing and full;

since the riches of the sea will flow to you,
the wealth of nations come to you;...

Your sun will set no more
nor your moon wane,
but Yahweh will be your everlasting light
and your days of mourning will be ended.

Your people will all be upright,
possessing the land for ever;
a shoot that Yahweh has planted,
his handiwork, designed for beauty.
                                    (Isaiah 60:4-5, 20-21 JB)

Inspired by such a vision of a new Jerusalem, the prophet
Haggai reminded the exiles who were returning to the city that
God alone is absolute. All else is relative. They naturally wanted
to be more practical, to build their own houses and then rebuild
the temple. But Haggai reminded them that if they honored
Yahweh above all things, he would be their shelter and their
protection. (Haggai's ministry and the work of the other Jewish
leaders to restore the temple and rebuild the walls of Jerusalem
are also desribed in the historical books of Ezra and Nehemiah.)
    Nevertheless, despite all their efforts, when the Jews
looked upon the rebuilt temple, they were disheartened.
Because of their poverty, they could not match the magnificence
of the former temple, the one built by Solomon. Through Haggai,
however, the Lord reminded them that the true glory of the
temple was not its gold or silver but his own presence residing
in it. This message speaks to us as well, when we get so caught
up in trying to make our churches look beautiful and forget that
their true glory is not in how fine and grand they look but in
the spirit of God, the spirit of the people who worship there.
The glory of the Church is never the work of our hands but the
handiwork of God.
    The last theme or image which appeared in the writings
of the prophets was that of the messiah. When Christians hear
that word today, they think naturally of Jesus. The name *Christ*
means in Greek "the anointed one," just as the Hebrew word
messiah means "the anointed one." So *Jesus Christ* means literally

"Jesus the messiah" or "Jesus the anointed one." But the Jews at this point in history were not thinking about Jesus as such; they did not know how God's plan of salvation would ultimately be fulfilled.

During the fifth century B.C., after the return from exile, prophets such as Zechariah and Malachi began to hope for an even greater restoration of Israel. Even though they were back in their homeland, they were still a poor people, living under foreign domination. They began to hope that Yahweh would come himself, or at least send someone anointed with his spirit, to give them full freedom and complete the work of their salvation. Thus they began to hope for a messiah, an anointed one, and to dream about how he would appear:

> Rejoice, my people! Shout with joy, children of
> Israel! For look, your king is coming. He is
> triumphantly victorious, yet he humbly rides a
> donkey's colt. He will have nothing more to do
> with chariots and horses, instruments of war.
> He will banish bows and arrows from the land,
> proclaiming peace for all the nations. And his
> empire will stretch from sea to sea, even to the
> ends of the earth. (Zechariah 9:9-10)

Today we can easily see in this prophesy an image of Jesus as the messiah, establishing a kingdom of truth in this world and yet doing so nonviolently. But we see that with Christian hindsight after 2,000 years of reflection and prayer. Earlier prophetic insight could only see that God had not yet come in all his glory to establish peace and justice on the earth. So they envisioned it as best they could, and what they saw was Yahweh as a victorious king, triumphing over the enemies of Israel. It was not yet the full vision, but it was a glimpse of what was yet to come. The Jews, the remnant of Israel, were learning slowly, just as we all learn slowly to be attentive to the Word of God and to interpret it correctly.

The Jews had come a long distance from the days when they thought they heard God telling them to conquer Canaan and kill all its inhabitants. In the time since Joshua they had come to understand that God does not want to establish his Kingdom by violence but through the reign of justice in the world. Still, they saw this in their own way, by their own lights, and we cannot find fault with them for that. At this point they still held to their provincialism, thinking the messiah would be just for them and imagining that God would somehow set Jerusalem up to rule the world for him. They saw themselves becoming the greatest nation on earth at some time in the future.

In the Bible we find a corrective for this narrowness of vision. The Book of Jonah is probably the closest thing we have in the Scriptures to what we call today a short story. Even though it was not based on a real event in Israel's history, it was included in God's written revelation because of the universal message that it held for religious people in ancient times, and which it still holds for us today. It is the message that even though some people come to see themselves as God's chosen ones, this does not mean that God has not chosen others as well.

The story is about a Jewish prophet whom Yahweh sends to call the people of Nineveh to repentance. Jonah says to himself, "Yahweh is *our* God! Why should those pagans have the privilege of hearing his Word?" And so he resists this call from the Lord, but of course he can never run away from God. He tries to escape in a boat, but during a violent storm he gets thrown overboard. So Yahweh sends a big fish to swallow him up and spit him out on dry land. And where does the prophet find himself? On the shore of Nineveh, the very city where Yahweh had told him to go in the first place!

Grudgingly Jonah goes to Nineveh: "Well okay, Lord, if you insist! I guess I've got to do it." But he hopes they won't believe him. He doesn't want them to have the good news that Israel has, the news that the way of God is the way to life. But he goes to the center of Nineveh and preaches the Word the Lord has given to him. And, wouldn't you know, they believe it! The Ninevites repent and turn to God.

Jonah is furious! "What right does Yahweh have to give his Word to pagans, to share what rightfully belongs to the people of the covenant?" He sits down in the hot sun, boiling with anger. But Yahweh still looks tenderly on his reluctant prophet and makes a tall leafy plant sprout up right on the spot to give him some shade. So Jonah cools down a bit, but the next day he discovers that the plant has died; the leaves are all curled up. Now Jonah is doubly furious!

The inspired story ends with the Lord speaking to this prophet and saying, in effect,

> Jonah, who are you to say to whom I may be gracious? Who are you to say whom I may love? Did I not love you, even though you did not love me? Just as I gave life to this plant which lived only for a day, I give my love to whom I will. Why should you be angry if I am loving? Why should you be stingy if I am generous?

As always, the good news looks too good to be true. We complain that it cannot really be that easy. We believe we have to earn the love of God, or at least deserve it somehow. We want to restrict the infinite love of God to just ourselves, to just the law-abiding people, to just the ones who have the right religion or who attend the right church. But God keeps telling us through his prophets, through the inspired Word we call the Scriptures, and even in our hearts: "Do not place limits on my love. My generosity is unbounded. I love you not because of what you do but because I am love itself."

Yet down to our own time institutional religion still wants to corner righteousness for the "normal," the company people, the ordained, the sacramentalized, the churchgoers, the heterosexuals, and all those who supposedly pay their dues to the system. We are still good at creating and hating heretics. We are all unconverted Jonahs running from God and universal compassion.

Throughout the age of the prophets, from the beginning of the monarchy to the return from exile, the Lord was giving Israel his Word of Life. Invariably they made mistakes. Invariably they understood it only partially. But invariably they also realized that it was a contemporary Word. It was a Word given to them in their own moment of history, for their own situation, for their own lives. Inevitably that Word got written down. Inevitably it was bound into a religious tradition.

Inevitably it was institutionalized and made to look very uncontemporary. But if we allow the Word of God to speak to us through the words of his prophets, we can hear in our hearts the message he wants to speak to us.

The Heart of the Prophetic Message

At the center of the prophets' ministry is their awareness of the transcendent God: a God who is above all things and yet within all things. The presence of God cuts across all the boundaries of space and time, so there is never any place or event from which God is absent. The prophets' consciousness was filled with that awareness of God's presence, a presence which was inescapable once they became attuned to it. It was this compelling religious experience which made them so impatient with their contemporaries. Their prophetic insight came out of that experience, seeing the contrast between what God was doing in their heart and what people were doing in the world around them.

What God was doing in their heart was loving them to life. He was loving them, calling them, drawing them into himself. He had loved Israel to life when they were still a bunch of slaves. He was inviting them to life when he gave them his law to follow. He was calling them to life even when they were running away from him to other gods. He was drawing them to life when they had given up on life, in exile. In the prophets' own experience of the call to divine life, they could see that same pattern repeated over and over again in the history of their people. When Israel responded to God's call in trust and fidelity, they lived and prospered. But when Israel turned a deaf ear to God, they died and were defeated.

God's call to life was, at the same time, a call to love. We know that so well from the preaching of the gospel, but even in Old Testament times the prophets were hearing that call and heeding it. Drawn into the love of God, they loved Yahweh with all their heart and soul. They loved their own people, laying down their lives so that their people might return to the love of the Lord. With clear insight they saw that living in the love that

81

is God implies hospitality to strangers, charity to the poor, justice for the oppressed. Often they saw this love extending only to the people of Israel, but they were coming ever closer to the realization that God's infinite love extends to everyone.

The amazing thing about the message of the prophets is that it's so simple. When you first read through the prophetic books in the Bible, it all looks so complicated: pages and pages of prophesies about this, that and the other thing; here it's against idol worship and there it's in favor of justice; now it's death and destruction and then it's mercy and consolation. But when you read the prophets again and again, you begin to see the central insight which arranges all of the details into a single pattern. The insight is the love of God, experienced and lived.

The experience of God's love is a religious experience. It is an experience of grace, of overwhelming beauty, of unbelievable mercy. It is a gift of forgiveness, of approval, of acceptance despite our sins, despite our guilt, despite our nonacceptance of ourselves. To live in that love means to live in grace, to be gracious and merciful to others. It means extending them forgiveness and approval and acceptance despite their own sins and guilt feelings. It means loving them even when they don't feel guilty about the evil they are doing. As Jesus said, it even means loving our enemies.

The prophets stood in the heart of that experience, at the core of that insight. From that central vantage point they understood and judged everything that was going on around them. They were neither conservatives nor liberals but, at the same time, they were both. They were archconservatives with respect to God: He is absolute, only Yahweh is Lord, there are no other gods but the one God. Yet they were flaming liberals with little respect for human institutions: Government, religion—all of it can change; none of it is absolute.

In the same way the prophets were both radicals and traditionalists. They were radical believers in the Lord and radical lovers of his people. We can even say that they were radical traditionalists. Their penetrating insight saw into the heart of their own tradition, the tradition that went back to God's covenant with Israel, the tradition that went further back than their recent religious institutions. They reminded their people of God's fidelity to that covenant and they called them to be faithful to the Lord who gave it to them.

In our own day, if we call ourselves the people of God, we must be like those prophets. We too must be radical traditionalists: not hundred-year traditionalists, or even four-hundred-year traditionalists, but four-thousand-year traditionalists! Our religious heritage as Catholics spans two thousand years of Hebrew history and two thousand years of Christian history. If we live within that constant and coherent tradition, we find that we are freed from concern about more recent, shorter-lived traditions. If we find the heart of our own Judaeo-Christian tradition, we discover the true catholicity of the Catholic Church, its genuine universality for all places and times.

For prophetic Christians, as for the Israelite prophets, the distinction between conservative and liberal is meaningless. The only distinction that matters is between those who know the Lord and those who don't. There are conservatives who really know the Lord, love the Lord and give their lives to him, trust the Lord and serve him with all their hearts. At the same time there are conservatives who want to preserve their power and privilege, or preserve the rituals they are used to, or preserve the legalisms of the recent past. Likewise there are liberals who know and love the Lord, yet who seek change in the Church's policies and in government policies. But there are also liberals who neither know the Lord nor love God, who are trying to change the world for their own ends and purposes.

The prophets of Israel did not care if others looked on them as conservatives or liberals. They cared only for the Lord and for the Word God gave them to speak. To some they looked like conservatives, preaching that old-time religion. To others they looked like liberals, questioning the status quo.

The same is true of prophets in our own day. Martin Luther King was unpopular for being too liberal, for speaking out against racism and for the rights of oppressed minorities. Yet he was only being faithful to the call that God had given him to preach the gospel of freedom. And, like so many of the prophets, he was murdered. Mother Teresa of Calcutta can be admired by conservatives, and yet her radical care for the poor is rooted in the same love of Christ as the gospel poverty of Dorothy Day, who was hated by conservatives. Antiwar prophets are labeled as radicals even when they call us back to the ancient tradition of Christian pacifism. Antiabortion prophets are labeled as conservative even though what they proclaim is the radical love of God for all human life.

The prophets past and present first of all call us into that experience of God's love which radically alters our vision of ourselves and our outlook on life. Too often we are concerned about petty things which in the end do not really matter. Too often we waste our time on trivial pursuits while our lives and the world around us are falling apart. We continue to rearrange the deck chairs on the sinking Titanic, and we think we are doing something important. Even more ironically, we think we're doing something good for God.

What the prophets are saying is this: Let God do something good for us. Let God be God. Let the Lord be the Lord. Let God lead. Enter into the experience of his presence and his love; after that, it does not matter much what you do. But don't be surprised if you find yourself falling in love with your tradition. Don't be surprised if you find yourself wanting to radically change the way things are. Don't be surprised if what you thought was unimportant becomes suddenly important to you. Entering into the vision and the love of God alters our perception of reality.

And so the past is prologue. The prophetic conscience of the past becomes the prophetic consciousness of the present, if we open our minds and hearts to God. The people in the days of Micah were wondering about the right way to be religious, worrying about the correct performance of their rituals, concerning themselves with looking good. Insightfully, the prophet said to them:

> What is good has been explained to you. The Lord wants only this: that you act justly, love tenderly, and walk humbly with your God.
> (Micah 6:8)

CHAPTER FIVE

Genesis and Job:
God and Humankind,
Good and Evil

People naturally assume that an introduction to the Scriptures should begin with Genesis, since that is the first book in the Bible. Our reason for not treating it first is to emphasize the fact that Genesis is not a book of history or a scientific account of creation. It is not an eyewitness report of how the world and the human race began. Rather, it is a mythological portrayal of the relationship between the Creator and the creation.

Although many of the stories found in Genesis were passed down from generation to generation among the Israelites, they were not collected and put into their final form until after the exile, around 500 B.C. In the aftermath of their national calamity, the Jewish people realized that their heritage might indeed be lost if it were not written down, and their religious leaders were inspired to gather together many strands of their oral tradition and weave them into a continuous narrative. They attributed the authorship to Moses, meaning that the authority for the wisdom of this tradition goes back at least as far as Moses' time. But we do not know the actual names of the scribes who wrote it in the form we have today. They were less concerned with putting their names on their work than with preserving the wisdom of their religious heritage.

The religious questions they were wrestling with are questions which thoughtful people ask in every age: What is the meaning of life? Where does it come from? Where does it go? What is the relationship between God and humanity? Why is there evil in the world? Why do good people have to suffer? These questions were especially disturbing for the Jews after their return from exile. They thought they had known who they were and what God's purpose was for them, but now with their dreams shattered, they were forced to think again and think more deeply.

Some of them found answers to those questions in the ancient myths of their tribal past. These are the stories found in Genesis. There was another author during the postexilic period, however, who found the same truth within his own inspired imagination. He expressed his insight in a long poetic story about a man name Job.

Both Genesis and Job, therefore, look like factual stories, but actually they are pieces of wisdom literature. The part of Genesis which begins in chapter 12 with the call of Abraham has details woven into it which may indeed be factual, but the human facts were less important to the writers than the religious truths that they were trying to convey. The second part of Genesis is therefore something like a blend of wisdom and historical literature.

The other wisdom literature in the Bible is found in the books of Psalms and Proverbs, Ecclesiastes and Ecclesiasticus, Wisdom and the Song of Songs. Many of these books were attributed to Solomon, who was noted for his wisdom, but here again, authorship in the ancient world did not mean what it does today. It meant that the authority for these books came from the same source as Solomon's wisdom, that is, it was another way of saying that they were divinely inspired.

In this introduction to the great themes of Scripture we will not deal much with these other wisdom books. The great themes found in them are the same as the ones we have already seen arising out of Israel's history and the prophets' religious insight. We find those same themes in the books which are the subject of this chapter, Genesis and Job.

Genesis 1 to 11

Perhaps the most important thing to bear in mind when reading the first chapters of Genesis is that it is written not about the past but about the present. It is about the perennial present, the present that is always with us. The prophets spoke the Word of God in their own present time, and in doing so they spoke eternal truth, the Word which is as true for us today as it was for ancient Israel. In a similar way, the authors of Genesis wrote down the Word that came to them in their time, but in doing so they were putting into human words the eternal Word which speaks the truth for every generation. They were writing what is always true about God and human beings, about the goodness of the world, and about the sin which causes suffering.

The Book of Genesis contains not one but two creation stories. Genesis 1:1—2:3 gives an account of God turning chaos into order, creating man and woman at the end, and resting on the seventh day. The rest of chapter two tells a different story, beginning with the creation of man, then the creation of the world of nature, and finally the creation of woman. The ancient writers were not worried by the obvious differences between the two accounts. For them, both revealed the same inspired truth: that God alone is God, that everything else is his creation, and that everything which God creates is good.

We see this most clearly in the first creation story. On each day of creation God looks at what he has done and calls it good. On the sixth day he looks back over everything he did and says, "Yes, it's all very good indeed!" And on the seventh day he rests.

What does this passage tell us? First of all, it is not meant to tell us how the universe began. That is something for scientists to figure out. Rather it tells us that, however it began, God is responsible for it. We did not create the world. The world did not create the world. God is totally responsible for all of creation. That's the long and the short of it.

Put in theological terminology, the story is saying that everything is grace, everything is gift, everything comes from

87

God. He is the one who makes something out of nothing and gives it to us, not way back when, but here and now. He makes us what we are, and gives us to ourselves as his free gift. He gives us all of nature, both the natural universe and our own human nature, and all of it is good. All of it is to be enjoyed, if we can but receive it as his gift.

The second thing this passage tells us is that after God works hard for six days, he takes a break. The Jewish authors saw this as the divine origin of the sabbath rest, but even the idea of the sabbath had a deeper religious significance. The story tells us in so many words that when we overly assert ourselves day after day and never take a break, we are trying to outdo God. Not even God worked every day of the week!

God is the master of it all; everything is in his hands. If we work as though everything depends on us, we say, in effect, we don't believe that. We don't trust God enough to leave it in his hands. We think we have to do it all. We want to take over God's work and do it all ourselves. A few chapters later we see what happens when people try to outdo God; but here at the end of this first creation story we see a foreshadowing of that great theme which runs through all the rest of Scripture, the theme of resting in the Lord.

In chapter two of Genesis we are given the second story of creation. It emphasizes God's relationship to all human beings, represented by the figures of Adam and Eve. Both of these names are symbolic. *Adam* in Hebrew means simply "man" or "human." It is based on the word for earth or soil, showing the man's connection with the dust from which he comes and to which he returns. The name *Eve* comes from the word meaning "living," for she is symbolically the mother of all living people (Genesis 3:19-20). Adam and Eve therefore represent all human beings, the entire human race. And what the story depicts is not something that happened at a certain time long ago but something that is eternally true, even now. It is a mythological portrayal of the perennial relationship between man and woman and God.

Symbolically the story is saying that man cannot understand himself except in relation to woman, that woman cannot understand herself apart from her relation to man, and that neither can understand their humanity apart from God. Woman and man are incomplete without each other, and both are fully human only when they are in union with God. God gives them life, and their life together with God is paradise. That's the way it has always been, and that's exactly the way it is now. We understand fully who we are only when we are in a loving relationship with the Lord, when we acknowledge the breath of his spirit within us, and when we are grateful for the wonderful gifts which he has given us.

The state of paradise, living in union with God and in harmony with one another, is symbolized by the garden. When we are living in right relationship with God and others, we are at peace with ourselves and the world; in the garden, all of nature reflects this perfect harmony. This is the ideal; this is the way it is meant to be; this is what God wants; this is the way God originally intended us to live. And yet we know from our experience that this is not the way things usually are. What happens? How do we get thrown out of paradise? The biblical author expresses his inspired insight into the problem of our estrangement from God and from one another in chapter three, the story of the fall.

In the story the woman and the man disobey the Lord by eating of the forbidden fruit, and so they are thrown out of the garden. On the surface it seems so silly; why didn't God just give them a second chance? But the deeper meaning is the deepest truth: Whenever we fall out of right relationship with God and others, we no longer experience paradise. The breaking of the unity is the loss of the community, which is the sharing of life in honest, open companionship.

The Lord gives human beings everything they need, but he also asks them to trust him by not eating the fruit of one tree in the garden. They get the idea that they could become like God if they eat the fruit, and so they give in to the temptation to choose personal power over dependence on the Lord. As soon as they do that, however, they lose the power they had, they give up their ability to draw their strength from union with God. They see their nakedness, and they are ashamed.

This is exactly the situation that we find ourselves in when we are born. This is the "original sinfulness" of the human race.

We want to put ourselves first. We want to be independent. We don't want to admit our dependence on God. We don't want to face the fact that we are made in God's image, for the biblical image of God is complete self-giving, complete loving. God so loved the world that he created it. He didn't have to give human beings his life, but he did. He gave of himself by breathing his spirit into us. The truth is so simple, but it is too much for us. Instead, we run away from reality and find ourselves in a condition which is anything but paradise.

So it is not God who throws us out of paradise. We throw ourselves out of paradise by rejecting God's offer of a life of union, a life that comes through faith and forgiveness. Or, rather, we discover that we are already in a world which is not in harmony, a world in which human beings are already sinful. In this condition we are estranged from God and alienated from others. They are strangers, they are enemies, even though the biblical truth is that they are all our sisters and brothers since we share a common experience as creatures; one God is the parent of our humanity. We are even strangers to ourselves, looking for the meaning of our lives, seeking it everywhere except where life comes from. By behaving in this way, by living this lie, we inherit the original sin and pass it on.

One might think that this is all there is to it. In our Christian shortsightedness we have sometimes even looked back in history only as far as Christ to see the union of God and humanity perfectly realized. But the inspired author says no, that is not the whole story; that is only the beginning of it. For before Adam and Eve leave the garden, Yahweh promises that human beings will recognize the lie for what it is, and they will crush its source (Genesis 3:15). They will overcome the temptation and defeat the tempter. Humankind will be victorious. The children of the earth will once again be the children of God.

The biblical writer realizes that this day is still a long way off. Yet still he recognizes the pattern of God's interaction with people's, the pattern of God's self-offering and people's rejection of union, and God's giving of life again and again and again. It is the pattern which underlies the story of Cain and Abel, of Noah and the flood, of the tower of Babel.

Within a short time, then, brother is killing brother. Separation from God brings alienation from others, and this is symbolized by the ultimate aloneness of murder, the cutting off of all communication. So Cain slays Abel, and in doing so he becomes estranged from everyone else as well. Still, he lingers on. His children live after him, as do the other descendents of Adam and Eve. Some know the Lord, but most do not. Alienation, competition and corruption cover the face of the earth.

In Genesis 6—10 the author of Genesis inserts a parable of good and evil. The story of Noah and the flood is similar to other ancient myths in the Middle East, where periodic flooding sometimes wrought unexpected destruction. It is the way of storytellers to draw a lesson from such catastrophes, and in the oral tradition of the Hebrews the flood grew into a universal lesson of human evil and divine goodness.

If you've ever been in a flood, you know that it's chaotic. The orderliness of life is destroyed; everything you've worked for is wiped out. The same happens in our lives when we don't live in right relationship with God and others. The harmony of life is destroyed; everything we've worked for becomes senseless. The great flood therefore symbolizes the natural consequence of evil. It happens all the time. The biblical author had seen it happen to Israel in the destruction of the kingdom. In this story he shows it happening all over the world.

Amidst this sinfulness and social chaos, however, there is one man who trusts in the Lord. The Noah story is a beautiful image of faith. Long before the full consequences of human evil are apparent, Yahweh tells him to build an ark. Imagine building this huge boat in the middle of the desert! But Noah trusts in God. He's been trusting in the Lord all his life, and his action is a natural consequence of his faithfulness. His neighbors laugh at him, but he still builds the boat. He builds it large enough for his family and hordes of animals; there is enough life in the ark to begin anew when the time comes. Then all heaven breaks loose, and human wickedness reaps its own self-destruction. The evil of the world is washed away, but those who know the Lord are saved. Faith is the ark of salvation.

The story ends with God renewing the face of the earth.

The slate has been wiped clean, and the human race has been given another chance. The animals come out of the ark and creation is re-created. Chaos has been replaced by harmony. God's commitment to humanity wins again.

As if that were not enough, God makes a covenant with Noah and his descendents. It is a rather primitive covenant, but it's a precursor of things to come. It's setting the stage. It's revealing the divine pattern to human beings to the extent that they can comprehend it at this point. The people agree to not let murder go unpunished, as it was before the flood. In return, Yahweh promises to never again let the world be destroyed by water. Evil will never triumph as it did before. It is a promise made to all people of faith, even today. It is a covenant with Life itself, "all living things." God loves life and alone has power to decree death.

You would think the human race would learn after that, but the biblical author knows better. Things may not be as bad as they could be, but they're still bad. How did they get that way? Well, for one thing, he knows that God has no grandchildren. Noah was a son of God, but not all of his children have that same closeness to the Lord. Slowly sin creeps in again, especially pride and self-sufficiency. The author also has a literary problem: If all human beings are descendants of Noah, how is it that they speak different languages? His literary answer draws upon another myth, the tower of Babel.

In chapter 11 we see a replay of the sin of the first two humans, this time reenacted on a grand scale. It is the drive for power, the desire for self-sufficiency. The people of the earth want to make a name for themselves instead of honoring the name of God, and so they decide to build a tower that will reach up to heaven itself. They start on the project, but then the Lord looks down and says, "Good grief, they're at it again! What can I do this time to teach them?" So he confuses their speech, and since they now speak different languages they have to leave their work unfinished. Eventually they scatter over the face of the earth.

The analogy is clear. People are always trying to make it on their own, to solve their own problems, to be like God. We do it with political and military alliances. We do it with economic policies and social oppression. And yet so often our desire for cooperation leads to competition, our striving for unity leads to disunity, our yearning for success leads to failure. Whenever some group thinks they have it all together, they alienate other people, and the struggle for power within the group itself leads to dissension and disintegration. That's because it's the human way, rather than the divine way. Only God's way leads to salvation. Only by discovering and participating in the divine plan can we accomplish what we want; and the divine plan is not the way of self-assertion but the way of self-surrender.

The same is also true in religion. We do our thing on Sunday and we think we're getting somewhere. We organize all kinds of parish and diocesan programs, and we believe we are accomplishing something. Not that liturgies and programs are bad in themselves; but we can look upon them as things we're doing for God, instead of allowing God to work in us through them. Even theology can be a human failure. We study and learn, and we debate and dialogue, and when we get some measure of agreement we think we're getting somewhere. But in the end, mere theologizing doesn't satisfy. It's talking about God rather than communicating with God, and unless our study of the Scriptures and our analysis of the doctrines leads us into a personal relationship with the Lord, it's just another word game. It's no better than an elaborate crossword puzzle. We think we want solutions to our religious problems and answers to our theological questions, but really what we want most deeply is divine life. But only God can give that to us, by leading us into union. All we can do is trust and receive a life of union, and then act from that center.

Genesis 12 to 50

And so the stage is set. In the mythological history of the opening chapters of Genesis, the inspired author has shown humankind again and again trying to accomplish their own salvation. Now it is God's turn. Or, rather, now in the unfolding of the story of divine redemption it is time to introduce a cast of characters who will allow God's plan to become visible.

The writer of this book already knows that God's salvation has a history; he is living in the midst of it. But it had to begin somewhere. In a truly historical sense it probably began with the escape from Egypt, which is why we began with the Book of Exodus. But in a truly religious sense, that could not be the actual beginning, not if God is God, not if Yahweh has been creating and redeeming from the very beginning. So the biblical author reaches back into the prehistory of Israel, to the time before the Exodus, to the time before the Hebrews, to a time of memory wrapped in legend, to the stories of Abraham and Isaac, Esau and Jacob, Joseph and his brothers.

We always look at the past from the perspective of today. When we Americans think of the founding of our nation, we look back at Washington, Jefferson, Adams and the other founding fathers. But if England had succeded in quelling the colonists' revolt, historians would have written about other men instead. When we think of the Civil War, Abraham Lincoln immediately comes to mind. But if the South had won the war we might first think of Jefferson Davis instead.

It is the same with Israel. From the historical perspective of the downfall of the Israelite kingdom, from the religious perspective of God's covenant with his people, and from the prophetic perspective of the need of trust in the Lord, the biblical author looks back to Israel's beginnings and sees clearly now that it all began with one man's faith.

When you are led in a direction you'd sooner not go, it is often the Lord's doing, not yours. And when you follow that lead and discover that your desires have been fulfilled in ways you never expected, you can be sure it is the Lord who was calling you to that place all along. That's the fundamental experience of faith. It's not having the right religion or the right doctrines or the right theology; it's having the right direction in life. It's going where the Lord is leading you. It's being open to that call, trusting it, and following it to new and unexpected life.

From the beginning of chapter 12 onward, the whole Book of Genesis is about faith, about answering God's call, and about trusting in the way God is leading. It's about self-abandonment and God-discovery, which are the same.

It begins with Abraham, or Abram as he was first called.

The name in Hebrew is related to *abba*, which means "father."
And so Abraham is the great forefather, the father of the
Israelites, the father of their faith. Yet Abraham was not an
Israelite or a Jew, and much less was he a Christian or a Catholic.
He never prayed in a temple; he never went to Mass. Still, he
had faith; and St. Paul tells us that Abraham's faith made him
upright in the eyes of God (Romans 4). Why was that? It was
because he listened to the Lord and followed his lead. He entered
into that relationship of trust with a personal God, that attitude
which we call faith. He left what was certain for what was only
a promise.

We read in the Scriptures:

> Yahweh said to Abraham, "Leave your country,
> your father's family and the people you grew
> up with, and go to the land I will show you. I
> will make you the father of a great nation. I will
> bless you and make your name famous, and you
> will be a blessing to many others."
>
> (Genesis 12:1-2)

The way of the Lord is always the way of promise. God steps
into a person's life and makes a promise. The person of faith is
the one who accepts that promise and expects it to be fulfilled.
So Abraham, the model of faith, packs up his family and sets
out across the desert.

Certainly that takes faith. But the biblical author is not
content with that. He wants to show that Abraham's faith is
extraordinary in a way that no one could possibly miss.
(Remember, the author is writing about faith, not about a factual
figure in history, and so he paints the picture in bold strokes.)
Not only does Abraham get up and go, but he's already 75 years
old! Not only that, but his wife Sarah is just about as old! And
not only that, but she is childless, sterile! How could she possibly
become the mother of a great nation? So the author is telling us,
in so many words, that this is faith! This is what it means to
trust in the Lord and scorn the consequences.

Faith has nothing to do with common sense. There's no
commonsense reason for Abraham to believe the Lord. Still, he

gets to the promised land, the future land of Israel, just as Yahweh promised. The Lord promised that the land would be there, and it was. After he reaches it, Abraham looks around and sees that the land is already populated, and that the local kings are always fighting to defend their territory. But he hears the Lord speaking to him again: "Don't worry for I am your shield" (Genesis 15:1).

So faith is the opposite of fear. The way of faith is the way of trust, relying on God to do the fighting, letting the Lord provide the protection. Still, Abraham is new at this faith business. So when God says to him, "I am Yahweh who brought you out of the city of Ur to give you this land as your inheritance," Abraham asks, "How can I be sure that you will give it to my descendants?" (Genesis 15:7-8).

Yahweh's reply is a classic invitation to deeper faith. Abraham's faith is great, and yet it must be greater still. God offers no proofs. Instead he tells Abraham to offer a sacrifice, which was the ancient ritual for entering into communion with God. In other words, the Lord simply invites Abraham to walk more closely with him. We know the Lord in the act of loving him, trusting him, being united to him. There are no logical proofs. There are no crystal balls. You know the Lord will fulfill his promise the same way you know a friend will keep his word: He looks into your eyes and you see in his heart that it will be done.

But how? That's Abraham's next big question. How will he have children from a wife who by now is 90 years old and sterile? He figures the Lord must be waiting for him to do something. So following the tribal custom of that age, he has a son, Ishmael, by a slave girl. But the Lord says, "No, you don't have to do a thing except be a husband for Sarah. It's not you who is doing this, but me. Trust me." So Abraham trusts the impossible and, sure enough, Sarah bears a son, Isaac. At last it looks as though the promise is coming true!

Still, Abraham's faith is not yet perfect. There is one more test. A few years later, Yahweh comes to him and says, "Okay, Abraham, I want to see how much you trust me. I want you to kill Isaac in sacrifice to me." But by now Abraham is ready for anything. He has seen God do the impossible before, and so he replies, "All right. You are the Lord. You know the promise. I still believe in the promise and that it will be fulfilled, somehow. If you say I must kill my only son, I'll do it." Faith is not always logical and sometimes it might even appear to be immoral at first sight.

Abraham leads his son up the hill and lays Isaac on the altar. He is doing something that his father's heart rebels against. He is about to do something that goes against all common sense. Then, just as he raises the knife, when he has trusted to the bitter end, the Lord says, "Lay down the knife. Don't harm the boy. Now I know for sure that you revere God, for you have not withheld anything from me, not even your only son" (Genesis 22:12). And so the Lord provides an animal to sacrifice instead. The Lord gives Abraham what he needs to enter into communion with him, since Abraham has given all he needs to give in order to enter into communion with God: He has given everything.

Thus Abraham becomes a free man. He was set free from family and country when he left his native land. He was set free from fear when he walked into hostile territory. He was set free from doubt when he let the Lord give him a son. Now he is set free from his ties to his own children and from worrying about the future because he has put himself entirely in God's hands.

And what does God do? He gives it all back to him. Abraham has a family again, he has a country again, he has a son again, he has a future again. The reward of his faith is freedom, the freedom to fulfill the deepest desire of his heart. That's the desire which the Lord puts there, the desire which leads to faith, just as faith leads to the greatest human fulfillment.

So Abraham dies a happy man. He has not seen his descendants. He has not seen the promised land become his own. But he has seen the Lord, and in that vision, he has seen it all.

In the remaining chapters of Genesis, the biblical author tells the story of Isaac and his two sons, Esau and Jacob, and of how Jacob wrestles with Yahweh and is given the name Israel. He tells the story of the 12 sons of Jacob, the fathers of the 12 tribes of Israel, and the story of how they go to Egypt to avoid a famine in Canaan. He tells the story of Joseph, the favorite son of Jacob, who trusts in God and saves his family from starvation. In a real sense, however, it is all the same story. It's the story of Abraham. It's the story of faith. It's the story of Isaac's faith and Jacob's faith and Joseph's faith as they follow the lead of the Lord.

Sure, they are not perfect. Jacob is a con artist and a real wheeler-dealer. But in the end he learns to trust the Lord. His sons are jealous of their brother, Joseph, so they sell him into slavery. But in the end they learn that God can redeem even their sin, and they find themselves saved from starvation because of Joseph's trust in the Lord. So the story of Genesis from Abraham to Joseph is the story of abandonment and fulfillment, and of how God is faithful to his promise whenever people trust in him, and even when they don't. It is the story of faith told over and over again, now with one cast of characters and now with another. And it is the story of the reward of faith, which is the fulfillment of the promise, but almost always in other ways than originally expected.

Job

The Book of Genesis has a happy ending. In fact, it has a number of happy endings, since every time Abraham and his descendents trust in God, things turn out well.

But that isn't true to life! Sometimes people trust in God and they wind up miserable, don't they? Sometimes other people don't give a damn about God, and they drive Cadillacs and retire in comfort. What's going on here? Who's the Bible kidding? That's the problem that the author of the Book of Job is wrestling with.

During the postexilic period when this book was written, the Jews did not believe in life after death (and most Jews, even today, do not). Judaism was and still is a this-worldly religion. Jews believe that the way to walk with God and to know the Lord is to be a full person, here and now, and they do not expect that to happen in another world after this one. In Judaism, there is no pie in the sky when you die; there is no prize in heaven for running the race on earth.

The logical consequence of this kind of thinking is that rewards and punishments have to come in this world, not in the next. Good behavior will be rewarded and evil will be punished by God, not after death but during life. Over and over again, in the Book of Proverbs and in other wisdom literature, the Hebrew Scriptures promise that the upright will prosper and the wicked will suffer the consequences of their evil ways.

All well and good. As long as things went relatively well for the Israelites, they could get along fine with this fairly simple moral theology. But then their kingdom was destroyed and the whole nation was led away into exile. Suddenly the system wasn't working any more! Something seemed terribly wrong with this simple theology of good and evil. Not only the guilty but also the innocent were suffering. Not only were the wealthy idol worshipers defeated, but the righteous poor were also being persecuted.

In the face of this unexplainable suffering, the Jews had to rethink their moral theology. The author of the Book of Job was wrestling with the mystery of evil, wondering how bad things can happen to good people, wondering if God truly loves the just and hates the wicked. Unlike modern theologians, however, the ancient writer composed his theology in poetry, and he wrote it in the form of a story or drama.

If we look at this book as a drama or play, we can easily see Job as the protagonist, God as the hero, and Satan as the villain. Job's three friends set the stage and keep the drama going. One after another they look at all the traditional solutions to the problem of evil and find them wanting. In the end, God interrupts the dialogue and gives the answer which leaves all the intellectuals at a loss for words.

In the opening scene Job is presented as an innocent and faithful servant of the Lord. He has led an upright life, treating others justly, and he has enjoyed good health and prosperity. At the beginning, therefore, the traditional theory that good behavior is rewarded and bad behavior is punished seems to be working.

Now Satan, being the devil's advocate that he is, goes before the throne of God and argues, in effect, that Job is being good not because he loves the Lord but only because of the reward he gets from being so law-abiding: "Sure, Job has been just and honest," says Satan. "Of course, he gives thanks to God every day. But that's only because you've blessed him. Take everything away from him and see if he still praises you!"

But the Lord has confidence in Job. He lets Satan take away everything that Job has—his wealth, his children, even his health. Still, Job refuses to curse the Lord:

Naked I come from my mother's womb. Naked
shall I return to the earth. The Lord gave, and
the Lord has taken away. Blessed be the name
of the Lord! (Job 1:21)

And so the stage is set for the drama which is about to unfold. For the rest of the book, Job confronts the mystery of evil. He bewails his misfortunes. He is tempted to give in to easy explanations for them. But he resists the temptations, and so he struggles with the apparent absurdity and meaninglessness of life.

Sooner or later everyone who tries to be good and do what is right reaches that same point. We have to struggle with the mystery of evil, the mystery of God, the mystery of life. But it is only by struggling with the mystery that we get to really know it. It is only by experiencing evil that we begin to appreciate it. It is only by wrestling with the Lord, as Jacob did, that we begin to learn that God is the source of our strength and deliverance. It is only by encountering life and letting ourselves be hit in the face by it, so to speak, that we even begin to comprehend what life is all about.

Hearing of the hard times that have befallen Job, three friends come to offer him sympathy and consolation. Eliphaz, Bildad and Zophar are their names—but some friends they turn out to be! They are the ones who tempt Job not to face what is really happening, to give up trying to comprehend it, to stop wrestling with God and just accept the ready-made answers that their culture and religion offer. They want answers and closure and consolation not soul-searching journeys.

Eliphaz speaks first. He tells Job to pray to God for help, because God always answers prayers. God rewards the just and punishes the wicked, and so if we get right with God, he will straighten out our life. Bildad reinforces this by pointing out that since Job is suffering, he must have done something to deserve it. What Job has to do, therefore, is confess his sinfulness to God and everything will be all right. Zophar finishes the argument with the idea that there is a definite cause and effect relationship between a person's action and God's response. God's justice would not let Job suffer unless there were some reason for it. These are all good religious answers. These guys would be outstanding members of the Holy Name Society or the local prayer group.

Undoubtedly these three comforters try to do the right thing. They try to point out to Job where he went wrong. They try to help him understand what secret sin is causing him this misery. And Job honestly tries. He tries to look at things their way. He tries to figure out where he went wrong so he can set it straight. But he cannot find the sin which his traditional religion tells him has to be there.

What's happening is that the neat religious system, represented by the three comforters, is breaking down. They are trying to force reality into their categories, but Job is dealing with reality on its own terms. They are trying to say what God is and how God has to act, but Job is struggling with the reality of God as he experiences it. They are talking about the problem of evil as something to be solved, but Job is struggling with the mystery of evil as something to be lived. They give intellectual answers which temporarily satisfy the mind, but Job is living at the gut level, where the answer has to be experienced in order to be known.

Let's not fool ourselves. Sure, we'd all like to identify with Job since he is the protagonist; he is the good person who patiently bears his pain. But really, all of us have often acted more like Job's three friends. And for so long Catholicism was like that. We had our catechism which told us all about God and the Church. We had our neat definitions which told us what was real and what wasn't. We had our moral prescriptions which told us right from wrong. We had our Roman Curia to solve our moral dilemmas.

As we begin to encounter the Lord in the Scriptures,

however, we discover that reality, even religious reality, is not so cut and dried. We find the Gospels telling us that the Spirit is like the wind (John 3:8). It comes and goes from where we do not know. We cannot control the Spirit. Our finite minds cannot comprehend the infinite God. We always want to capture God in words, but God will not allow that. The experience of God will not allow that. This is what Job is discovering. This is what the scriptural author is dealing with by writing the story the way he does.

With Israel's exile still fresh in his mind the biblical author confronts the mystery of suffering, pushes hard against it and refuses to be satisfied with pious platitudes. And he begins to suspect that there is something more. Because he has seen the old reality breaking down, because he has witnessed the breakdown of the old morality, he starts to wonder whether the answer can even come in this life. There is almost a longing for immortality in his soul. Job expresses this longing in chapter 14:

> There is hope for a tree, that if it is cut down,
> it will start its life again. Though its roots are
> old and its stump decays, it can sprout new
> branches from the ground. But if a man dies and
> is buried, where is he? As water disappears into
> the air and into the earth, the spirit of a man
> drains from his body, never to return. If only
> you could hide me in Sheol, sheltering me there
> until your anger had passed, then remember me
> and call me back to life!
>
> Once a man is dead, can he come back to
> life? If it were so, I would serve out my time and
> wait for my release to come. Then you would
> call and I would answer you, knowing that you
> wanted to see me once again! (Job 14:7-15)

Job is hoping against hope, believing against everything he has been taught to believe. The author senses that there's something more to life than what appears. As a nation, the Israelites have seen themselves defeated and dead in exile, yet a remnant still survives and carries with it the hope of rebirth.

As an Israelite, the author wonders whether what they have experienced in their corporate life might also be possible in individual life. Could there really be a way to survive after death, a place where God's justice will be truly realized? In one passage at least, the author of Job seems confident that there is:

> I know that my redeemer lives, and in the end
> he will take his stand upon the earth. After this
> body has decayed, these eyes will look upon the
> Lord, and I will see God close to me—not
> someone else, but him! My heart trembles at the
> thought! (Job 19:25-27)

In this passage Job takes the leap of faith. He has walked with the Lord this far. He knows he's suffering. He knows his life is meaningless. Yet in the experience of the Lord he has found meaning, he has touched on something real, something that seems capable of going on forever. And so he believes in it, in that space where faith and hope are mixed together, resting in the wordless confidence of a felt promise. He trusts that his walk with the Lord will continue even after death.

Still, Job's faith does not eliminate his suffering. For chapter after chapter he wrestles with the mystery of suffering. He has hoped for justice and redemption, but he can only hope. Then, in chapters 29 to 31 he restates his case, protesting his innocence in the grip of undeserved, incomprehensible misery. He begs God for an answer. He almost blasphemes, calling God cruel and heartless. He even demands a hearing, as if hoping that God will be provoked into coming out of hiding and give him the response that he longs for.

Which of us would dare to pray like that? And yet this is real prayer. It comes not from the mind and lips but from the heart and gut. He knows where he stands with God. He knows he's done nothing to deserve what he's gone through. He has trusted God all his life, so now he trusts that God will read his purity of heart even if his words sound presumptuous.

We can never presume too much of God. We can never ask too much of God. How could we ever make God too big? How could we ever trust him too much? How could we ever ask him to love us too much? God is always more than we think. God always loves us more than we expect him to.

In his suffering, with his hope of resurrection, Job's journey becomes a symbol of the Calvary that every person of faith eventually must climb. It's an experience that we all have to go through. The important thing is that, like Job, we do not run away from it. We need to face it, even though we'd rather not face it, and go through it. For it is by going through, living the mystery, that we find salvation. It is in the crucifixion that we discover resurrection. It is by the letting go of life that we are set free to live.

Chapter 32 introduces a new character to the drama, a young man name Elihu. He explains that he held himself back while his elders were speaking, but now he would like to have his say. In fact, despite his youth, Elihu shows he has a rather mature attitude toward suffering. Spiritual wisdom is not a function of age; adults can sometimes learn a lot from kids. Rather, spiritual wisdom comes from living with and thinking about suffering. Children who have suffered a lot are sometimes more mature than grown-ups who have not.

This, in fact, is Elihu's theme. Suffering leads us into spiritual growth, if we take it in the right way. It helps us to reexamine our life and motives, if we allow it to purify us. People who have experienced a great deal of undeserved suffering in their lives often reach a depth of wisdom and a quality of patience and an ability to love which is refreshing when you find it. They don't make demands on you; they are ready to accept you as you are. They don't go through life wanting people to serve them; they look for opportunities to help others. They are not very possessive about what they own; they regard everything they have as a gift.

Yet suffering does not automatically have this effect on us. A lot of people are embittered by suffering; their personality shrinks, and they become small-minded and self-centered as a result of their experience. So it is not what happens to us that matters so much as our attitude and response to it. And it is only the response of faith, and self-abandonment, that sets us free. It sets us free from worry about the past and anxiety about the future. It sets us free from licking our wounds and wanting revenge. It sets us free to see reality for what it is, instead of looking at it distorted by our own pain. It sets us free to live every moment to the fullest. This is true liberation of the spirit, and it often only comes through suffering, through having everything you depended on taken away from you. We are free from fear to the degree that we are free from self.

When everything you thought you needed to be happy is taken away, only then are you in a position to find happiness without it. Sometimes when the Lord is all you've got, you discover that the Lord is all you need. But that's not something you learn by hearing it or reading it; that's something you learn only through experience.

And so in chapter 38 Job hears the Lord speaking to him amid the chaos of his life. His heart is confused by the way life has knocked him around, and his head is spinning with all the advice he's been getting. But in this whirlwind Job experiences God; and out of the tempest the Lord finally speaks to him.

What Job hears is not comforting. At least it does not sound too comforting to someone who has not experienced it for himself:

> Where were you when I created the earth? Tell
> me, since you seem to know so much! Who
> decided to make the world the way you see
> it?...Have you ever told the morning to break
> out into day?...Do you know where the light
> goes when it gets dark?...Have you ever seen
> the place where snow and hail come from?
> ...Have you ever made it rain?...Can your voice
> thunder across the sky?...Did you build the
> mountains or dig the valleys?...Did you decide
> what animals would roam the earth, or how they
> should behave? (Job 38—39, passim)

God goes on and on, describing all the goodness of creation. Job is blown away by the insight that his wisdom cannot begin to compare with God's:

> Compared to you, I don't know anything! What

can I say? I'd better just shut my mouth. I tried
to say things before, but there is nothing I can
say now! (Job 40:4-5)

Then God reminds Job that everything, absolutely
everything is in his control, not only the good, but also the evil
in the world. Even when wickedness is monstrous, even when
human beings cannot comprehend it, the Lord understands
what is happening.

In effect, the Lord is saying to Job, "I am God, and you
are merely human. That is my reply." And that is all the answer
God will give him. "I am God and you are human. Who are you
to say I am not loving?" That's the insight of faith. That's the
insight that comes from the overwhelming experience of God's
goodness. It gets purified and refined in the experience of
suffering and deprivation, until nothing remains but the
realization that God's love surrounds us even in our nakedness.

And so Job bows his head before the mystery of God:

I realize that you can do anything, and that
nothing can stop you. All my foolish words
cloud the issue; I lost sight of your providence.
I was talking about things I didn't understand,
marvels beyond my comprehension....Before, I
had only heard about you, but now I see you as
you are. I take back everything I said, and in
dust and ashes, I repent. (Job 42:2-6)

What is Job doing here? He is allowing God to be God.
God is wholly transcendent, wholly beyond us. His infinite
wisdom totally surpasses our finite minds. If we can accept that
relationship we can be redeemed. It is not a slavish relationship.
Rather, by accepting that relationship we come into wholeness
and experience our holiness. When we enter that relationship
with the Lord we discover that we are not strangers in paradise,
for we find ourselves walking as friends in the garden with the
God who loves us. In this relationship, God is still God and we
are still ourselves. However, it is not an abstract relationship. It
is a real relationship, a personal relationship, a felt relationship.

And in the experience of that relationship we discover the meaning of our existence.

Victor Frankl in *Man's Search for Meaning* recounts how the Jews in Nazi concentration camps survived the horrors of their situation by finding a meaning that made life worth living, despite the physical and psychological torture they suffered. In most cases people found this meaning in the love they knew someone had for them. Living in that relationship of love kept them from committing suicide; it gave them a reason for living, it gave them purpose and direction and hope and a desire to go on in the midst of their deprivation. Frankl discovered in the 20th century what the author of the book of Job discovered 25 centuries ago, that the realization that we are loved saves us from being shattered when the world around us crumbles.

What the Book of Job is saying, in the end, is that God does not give an answer to the problem of suffering but he gives us meaning in the midst of suffering. Logic and reason cannot explain the mystery of evil. Nothing can ultimately explain why some people suffer more than others, and why good people often have to endure more than their share of pain and hardship. Most of the Book of Job is spent in debunking the pat and facile answers which are offered as explanations to those problems. But at the end it says that God does not give answers, God gives meaning—and in that God gives power.

Job accepts the truth, and he bows before the mystery of it. He repents, that is to say he undergoes a conversion in his mind and heart: from complaining about what he has lost to concentrating on what he is—a son of God. In the realization of his sonship he experiences the meaning of his existence, he discovers the meaning of his life. In the light of that discovery, everything else fades into the background. He is liberated from self-centeredness and self-justification, he is enabled to accept his humanness, and he is freed to accept life on its own terms. God alone is good. Everything we have is gift. The Lord gives and the Lord takes away. Once Job knows who he is, in the experiences of his relationship with God, he can go on. His life has meaning.

When we realize this, it is as though everything we lost comes back to us. In the story this is symbolized in the final verses by God giving back to Job everything he had at the beginning, and more. The poetic tale has a poetic ending.

The poetry of the Scriptures is in many ways more true to life than the abstractions of theology. Theologians speculate about the problem of evil and come up with intellectually respectable solutions to it. But somehow these answers do not touch us in our grief, they do not alleviate our pain. They can be written down and taught to others, but they do not often lead us to conversion. Perhaps that is because these answers come to us too easily. We only need to understand them with our minds.

Job's answer didn't come like that. He had to fight to find his answer. He had to struggle through his grief to find a living answer in the chaos of his life. He had to find the living Lord in the middle of the tempest. He searched and found a personal answer in his personal relationship to God. Each one of us has to find such a relationship in the suffering that we ourselves experience, be it the loss of a job or a home, the death of someone we love, rejection by our parents or our children, the breakdown of a marriage, institutional injustice, social violence or whatever. The causes of our personal suffering are many. And when we find the living, liberating answer that gives us meaning in the midst of suffering, we realize that it is a very personal answer.

That kind of answer cannot always be verbalized; it cannot always be written down; it cannot always be passed on to students or even to members of your own family. But it is an answer that you know. It is a conviction that is deep and all-pervasive. In it you find the security to be insecure. No one can give it to you; no one can take it away. It is a gift. It's what happens in the heart of the person who discovers and trusts in the Lord.

CHAPTER SIX

Salvation History:
Faith in Evolution

In this chapter we will take a look at the entire Old Testament and try to put it together within a single historical perspective: the history of salvation, or salvation history.

Christians sometimes used to say that the God of the Old Testament and the God of the New Testament were like two entirely different beings: a God of anger, on the one hand, and a God of love, on the other. As we have seen in the first five chapters of this book, however, Yahweh from the very beginning was a God of love and fidelity. He created a people and directed them toward a future which he alone could accomplish for them.

From the vantage point of the New Testament, we can see that the Lord was creating a people who would be able to say yes to God. Mary said yes to God, and God came fully into her life, even into her body, in the conception of Jesus. Jesus from the first moment of his existence was a fully human yes, completely open to the Father, and entirely filled with God.

The 11th chapter of the Epistle to the Hebrews looks at the whole development of the Old Testament as a history of faith, a history of people hoping for what they could not yet see but following confidently the lead of the Lord in the assurance that what they were hoping for would eventually happen. The chapter is too long to be quoted in its entirety, but we can summarize a good deal of it as follows:

It was because of their faith that our ancestors

became famous. Cain and Abel both offered sacrifices to God, but Abel's was acceptable because it was offered in faith. Enoch, we are told, so trusted in God that he was not allowed to die, but instead was taken right up into heaven. This reminds us that faith draws us closer to God; in fact, it is only by faith that we see him.

Noah's faith in what God told him about the coming flood led him and his family to be saved, even though they looked foolish to their unbelieving neighbors when they were building the ark. The call of faith led Abraham out of his homeland and into the land that God promised to his descendants. Sarah's faith enabled her to conceive a son even though she was past the age for childbearing. Abraham's faith was tested when he was asked to offer up his only son, Isaac. Isaac too was a man of faith, as were his son Jacob and Jacob's son Joseph.

All these ancestors died trusting in what the Lord had promised to Abraham without ever seeing that promised fulfilled. Yet they lived in faith, confidently believing that the Lord was leading them to a homeland. Today we know that he was really leading them to himself.

Moses could have had a comfortable life in the court of the pharaoh, but instead he chose in faith to suffer in solidarity with his people. He heard God calling him to free the Israelites from slavery; and when he led them out of Egypt across the desert, it was his faith in God that guided him. It was by trusting in God that the Israelites brought down the walls of Jericho and eventually conquered the promised land.

Similar things could be said about Gideon, Samson, Samuel, David and the prophets. It was their faith in God that enabled them to conquer their enemies, establish their kingdom, and even perform miracles.

But where does all this history lead up to? The author of the Epistle makes it clear:

Keep your eyes on Jesus, our leader in faith, and the one who brings it to perfection. For the sake of the joy which lay ahead of him, he was willing to endure a shameful death on the cross. And now he sits at the place of honor at the right hand of God's throne. (Hebrews 12:2)

What the Epistle to the Hebrews is saying is this: In the person and the life of Jesus, the revelation of the previous 2,000 years is brought to completion. All the written words of the Old Testament lead up to the personified Word in Christ.

Sometimes when we look at that revelation, it looks as though it has changed or evolved over the course of 2,000 years. But if God is a God of steadfast love, then it is not God who changes but we who change. God does not evolve except through us; people's experience of God, however, evolves, and their understanding of that experience evolves. It grows and deepens with every new generation as they move to deeper levels of commitment and vision. Evolutionary faith is an increasing trust combined with an increasing comprehension of what the journey of faith is all about. That is why we speak of the "development of doctrine."

We can see this illustrated in the history of Israel's salvation, which is the first part of Christian salvation history. But we also see it exemplified in the lives of individuals and the experiences of communities that are growing in faith. The pattern of growth in Israel's faith is the same pattern that we find in people's faith anywhere in history and anywhere in the world today. It is a universal pattern of faith development.

Evolutionary faith is not something that you have to believe in. It is something that you can verify in your own life. But it is something that you can only see in retrospect. Only from the vantage point of where you've gotten can you see how you got there, how the Lord was leading you from the beginning, and how the entire story was really a journey of faith. People who have never trusted in God or who are just starting out in the life of faith cannot see this, because they have not yet experienced it. But people who have experienced it eventually come to a point where they can begin to understand it, to see how the Lord was leading them from where they started out to where they ultimately got.

When they look back at their beginnings, people of faith can perceive the extraordinary in the midst of the ordinary. They can begin to see God's action in their lives, much the same as the Israelites looking back saw God's action in their history. But at the beginning, everything seems so ordinary. When St. Francis started out begging stones to rebuild a church, he didn't know that the Lord was leading him into the rebuilding of the medieval Church. When St. Benedict or St. Ignatius or Dorothy Day or Martin Luther King were starting out, they weren't sure where they were being led. Maybe they weren't even certain that God was calling them to found orders or to start movements. And certainly along the way there were dark periods when they did not know where they were going. Only later, when they looked back on their lives, did they see their paths illuminated and understand that the Lord had been there from the very beginning, leading them all the way through.

Perhaps the same is true in your life as it is in mine. Every day seems like an ordinary day. Why would anyone call it significant? Yet looking back over the past year, or three years, or 10 years, or 20 years, we can often see a meaning that escaped us at the time. We begin to see the significance of those insigificant days. Meaninglessness gets turned into meaning. Our past is redeemed in the light of our present salvation. That's what we mean by God's faithfulness and goodness to us: He is always saving us in spite of ourselves, even when we don't recognize it. When we do recognize it, we can see with the eyes of faith what we could not see before: We were being gifted from the very beginning, and God's grace was with us all along.

As we begin to recognize the journey of faith, we can also discern four stages, or levels, through which faith evolves:

In the first stage, people start to experience the reality of God and his love. Before this, very often, God has just been a name or a concept to them, but then somehow they encounter the Lord in their life and God becomes real for them. At the same time, however, they tend to believe that God's love is limited to just themselves, to a select few such as a chosen people or the one true Church.

In the second stage, people begin to respond to God's love, but they perceive God's love as dependent on their response. They believe that grace is a conditional gift, that God will love them if they are good, that God will save them if they keep the commandments. They think that God's covenant is an agreement that God will be gracious to them if they earn it, that they will get rewarded if they merit it.

In the third stage, people begin to see God's love as unlimited and unconditional, but they do not see further than that. They acknowledge that God loves them whether they are good or bad, and that he is gracious to the just and the unjust alike. But they think that God is doing that from afar, from up in heaven someplace. They do not yet see themselves as involved in the process.

Finally, in the fourth stage, they make the breakthrough to seeing that God's grace and love are incarnate in human lives and interactions. They perceive it first of all in God's incarnate Word, but then they realize that God acts through them in the same way. They experience God's love within, loving themselves and others and redeeming the world through them. But they realize that it is God who is doing the loving, God who is doing the saving; and they surrender themselves to being channels of God's grace in the world. They let go.

Three of these four stages can be seen in the Old Testament; the fourth can be seen in the New Testament. By the end of the Jewish revelation, the Israelites knew that they were a chosen people, that God had given them a covenant to live by, and some of the prophets were beginning to suggest that God's salvation even went beyond that. But it is only in the New Testament that the final breakthrough is made, as the good news was preached not only to Jews but also to Gentiles, and as the Church went beyond the boundaries of Palestine. The true meaning of Christian faith is therefore faith at this fourth level: a universalizing, truly catholic faith that transcends the boundaries of nationality and culture. At the same time, it is a personal, truly incarnate faith which is immanent in the life of every follower of Christ.

Looking back on the Christian past, however, it is clear that the institutional Church has lived much of its faith life at the second and even at the first level. Reward-and-punishment morality and the ethical system of obeying commandments in order to get to heaven—this is faith at the second level of development. Religious exclusivism, restricting salvation to members of the Church and denying it to those outside it—this is faith at the first level of development. Very often the Church has not really understood the revelation of the New Testament, for it has operated out of an Old Testament style of faith. And this is true today no less than it was in the past.

Let us now examine each of these stages, or levels, of faith in some detail.

Exclusive Faith

Going back to the beginning, we see that Abraham and his descendants, the children of Israel enslaved in Egypt, responded in faith to God's call to believe and trust. They felt God's election, they trusted God to lead them, and they saw God's action in their lives. So the positive side, the growth side, of this stage of faith is the experience of God revealing himself and the response of trust to this self-revelation. But this stage of faith also has a negative side, a restrictive aspect. The Israelites believed that God's love was limited just to them; they thought that God had elected them to the exclusion of others.

This kind of exclusive thinking results in what is sometimes called ethnocentric religion. It is characterized by a them-versus-us or an in-group/out-group mentality. The focus of this religion is on the in-group, the elect, the select few who know the truth and are saved. Excluded are members of the out-group, the pagans, the nations who do not know God and are therefore lost. This kind of religious approach soon becomes "righteousness" rather than true faith.

For people with exclusive faith, loyalty is the supreme

virtue. They are loyal to the leaders of their own religion, and they do not care very much about others. They try to keep themselves pure and separate from other groups with other religious beliefs. They perceive foreign beliefs as false and strange gods as a threat. They cling to symbols that identify them as the chosen ones, and they refuse to be contaminated by contact with ideas and practices which are different from their own.

We can see this style of faith in the religion of very young children. Very often they perceive what they are taught by Mommy and Daddy as true, but they cannot yet deal with the beliefs of others, so they exclude these from their consciousness. Their loyalty to their parents' values, or their Church's religion, is absolute. And although they may not in their youthful innocence fear other values, they do not know how to handle them, and they do not think about them.

In our own religious history, we do not have to go back very far to find our Church, or even ourselves as adults (if we are old enough to remember it), characterized by this kind of mentality. Until very recently it did not seem as important to be faithful to the Lord as to be loyal to our group—the Catholic Church, the ethnic parish, the religious order, or what have you. You could hear people say, "This is what good Catholics believe," or, "This is what good German Catholics do," or, "This is the way good Franciscans ought to behave." And, all too often, this is where it stopped. We preached Catholicism, or a nationalistic version of it, or some religious spirituality, instead of preaching the Lord.

From the perspective of the later stages of faith, we can see how limiting this religious mentality is. It is as though people resist hearing clearly the call of God because of the demands that it would make on them. The invitation to a deep and personal relationship with God involves constant listening and ego-stripping and complete surrender to the Lord. And so many people stop at this first stage (or regress to it, as the Israelites often seemed to) and conclude that all God expects of them is loyalty to the in-group. It's so much easier to believe that God wants us to do what everyone else is doing. Loyalty to the group is simpler than trust in God.

This we/they mentality naturally leads to the belief that since we are the chosen ones, others are not; or that since we are loved by God, others are not. And we feel this gives us a right to hate or even destroy what we think God does not love. From our study of the Scriptures, we can see that the primitive morality connected with this stage of religious faith led the Israelites to self-righteously slaughter those who were not like themselves. From our knowledge of Church history we can likewise see that in the Middle Ages this type of primitive morality led Christians to believe that torturing and burning heretics was justified, or that killing people by the thousands in crusades was something God approved of. And today many Christians are quite ready to push the button to protect their sacred explanations with nuclear warheads.

It was, as we can see now, a childish type of faith and a primitive type of morality. It was a beginning, to be sure, but it was and is *only* a beginning. At the very least, it is better than no faith and no morality. But it is not good to complacently remain there. It is better to listen more closely and to hear God's call to a deeper level of faith and a higher stage of morality.

Covenant Faith

When the Israelites followed Moses out into the desert, trusting in the God who freed them from slavery in Egypt, they knew that they were loved, that they were a chosen people. They were walking in the faith of their forefather Abraham, believing in their election by Yahweh. But Yahweh wanted to call them to a deeper faith, and at Mount Sinai, in the desert, the Israelites responded to that call by entering into a covenant with God.

Again, when viewed from a later perspective, we can see that God wanted more from them than covenant faith, but this is all that they could give him at the time, and God in his mercy was willing to love them where they were. God's love for the Israelites was never less than infinite, but they were not yet ready, not yet willing to hear that. And so instead they heard God's love being offered to them in terms of an agreement, a bargain, a deal. God's love for them was always unconditional, but they were only able to hear it as something conditional. If they would keep their part of the agreement by obeying the commandments Yahweh gave to Moses, Yahweh would protect them and lead them safely into the promised land. That was the deal. Or at least that's how they understood it.

When you have this kind of faith in God, you believe there is a sort of agreement that God will do his part if you will do yours. God will save you if you obey the commandments; and if you don't, he will punish you. It's a tit-for-tat mentality. You believe that if you're good, God will love you; and if you're bad, God won't. You think that there's a way to earn God's love, to merit the reward of heaven, and so morality becomes a matter of earning enough merits and avoiding enough demerits so that when you die you will be saved. You earn your merits by doing the right things according to the rules; you get demerits when you break the rules and commit sins.

This sort of faith can be very individualistic and very self-centered. Christians in the past have often talked about saving their souls, and priests were taught that their job was to help people save their souls. And how did people save their souls so that they might enter heaven? By obeying the commandments, by living according to the rules, by seeking perfection.

Catholics have been especially prone to this type of thinking. When I was in the Franciscan novitiate, I tried so hard to save my soul by being perfect! In the eyes of my religious superiors I was the perfect novice. I obeyed all the rules to the letter. I was never late for meals. I was never late for prayers. I stood when I was supposed to stand, and I knelt when I was supposed to kneel. When I bowed, I did it exactly the way that we were told to do it. Being such a perfect seminarian gave me a satisfied feeling of having my act together. It gave a sense of righteousness because I knew that I was obeying the law.

And yet I can see now that the focus of my attention was myself. I was not surrendering to the Lord. I was earning my own salvation. I had not yet learned to let God save me. I hadn't even learned the basic meaning of the Lord's name. *Jesus* means "Yahweh saves." Yet there I was, trying to save my own soul. Many of us in religion have been guilty of this type of attitude, stuck at this level of faith.

Quite obviously the central virtue at this stage is obedience: obedience to the commandments, obedience to the rules, obedience to religious superiors. In the Old Testament this is shown by the great proliferation of commandments in later Judaism. We Christians tend to think of only 10 commandments, but in later Judaism the scribes counted up all the do's and don'ts in the Bible and enumerated 613 commandments! The Pharisees believed that if they obeyed every jot and tittle of all these laws they would be perfect, just as I believed that I was perfect by obeying every little rule in the novitiate.

And many Catholics still have this mentality today. They think that being a good Christian means obeying all the commandments of God and obeying all the laws of the Church and obeying everything the pastor says. This is a religion of obedience. It's the religion of the Pharisees. Prayer, struggle and mercy are not really necessary.

And yet it's not all bad. Looking back, I must admit that I learned a lot and grew a lot during that stage of my development. Every child also goes through this stage in their psychological and their religious development. They become very rule conscious; they love to play children's games; and learning and playing according to the rules gives them a lot of enjoyment. When others break the rules, they become frustrated and even furious at times; they don't know how to handle it.

Religion at this stage is also a matter of learning and obeying the rules. And we can all see that if we never learned the basic rules of life, gaining respect for the law and living according to it, life would be chaotic, lawless and miserable for everybody. It's a stage we all have to go through and incorporate into our lives if we are to ever grow beyond it. I always say that it is best to *begin* conservative, but faith doesn't allow you to stay there. This type of faith is too self-protective and too self-satisfying, often blocking further growth. Growth in faith must progress *through* conservatism *to* liberation from complacency with the status quo. (This is one reason why Jesus was so hard on the law-abiding and the rich.)

Looking beyond the individual to society, then, we can

see how religion at this stage becomes a matter of obedience and ritual. The rules tell us how to behave, and if we always behave according to the rules our actions become rituals. There are little rituals and big rituals, less important and more important rituals. There are the social rituals of morality and the prayer rituals of liturgy. Breaking the lesser rules of morality are venial sins; breaking the greater moral laws are mortal sins. Bending the liturgical rubrics may make a liturgy illicit, according to canon law; violating important Church regulations in a liturgy could make it canonically invalid.

Rules and rituals such as these are necessary. We all have to learn them if we are to live together in peace and pray together in harmony. Yet if we become too rule-conscious and fixated at this stage, our morality can become legalistic and our worship can become ritualistic. We fall into a trap if we think we are earning salvation by obeying the laws, or if we believe that we are meriting grace by observing the rules in our rituals.

Looking at our own Church's history, we can see the inherent danger of becoming trapped at this stage of religious development. We identify faith with obeying the commandments and we identify worship with performing the correct rituals. Those who do not obey the rules or who do not worship the way we do are shunned, excommunicated, just as the Catholics excommunicated the Protestants four centuries ago.

By doing that, the Church became very provincial, restricted to certain parts of Europe instead of being the universal Church of Christendom. Just think of it: provincial Catholicism. What a contradictory phrase! Yet in our self-righteousness we preferred provincialism. It's the same self-righteousness that I experienced in my individualism while in the seminary.

At its worst this type of religion becomes a sort of practical paganism. People are nominal Christians, cultural Catholics, yet practical atheists. They do not really know the Lord; they are not allowing God to save them. They think that they are saving themselves, saving their own souls. They are tied up in a self-serving religion of practices, chained by their own fears and cultural prejudices. It makes them feel good, it makes them feel together. But it is only the illusion of goodness which comes

119

from going to Mass on Sunday, putting money in the collection basket, and doing other good things. It is only the illusion of togetherness from belonging to the right Church, sending their children to the right school, and doing what everybody else does. It is a very complacent form of Christianity, a very self-serving form of Catholicism. It is sure that it is right, and because it is so sure, it has no need for the God of the Scriptures, the God who calls us out of ourselves to love those who are different from us, to recognize ourselves in our would-be enemies.

If there is a God for people who are fixated at this level, it is a God of judgment and order. He is the great policeman in the sky, keeping track of everything that people do and say. He is even a God of vengeance and a God of war, justifying the punishment of those who break the rules and approving the suffering which the righteous inflict upon the wicked. One could argue that this type of God is better than no God at all. And yet, from the perspective of the Scriptures, it is worse. The corruption of the best is always the worst. In comparison to the God who revealed himself to the prophets and the God who revealed himself in Jesus, this is a false and hollow image. It is an idol. The God who is the Lord, the God who truly is God, can only be seen with the eyes of a deeper faith.

Prophetic Faith

As we have seen in the earlier chapters, it was the prophets who first realized that the Israelites' conception of God was far too limited. Today when we look back over the earlier books of the Bible, we can see that the God of the postexilic prophets was the same God who was revealing himself from the beginning. When the Hebrews were first coming to know the Lord, however, they believed that Yahweh was just the God of their nation and that God's love for them was dependent on their keeping the commandments. It was not until after the kingdom was destroyed and they realized that temple worship was not as important as the worship of the heart that they understood that God's love for them was not dependent on their ability to live up to the demands of the law.

That realization—that God unconditionally loves both the good and the bad, that he lets his rain fall on the just and the unjust alike—was a breakthrough to a new dimension of faith. The later prophets and the wisdom writers who were listening to what God was revealing to them through the disasters which befell the kingdom were the first to discern this. They discovered that God was with them in their suffering as well as in their triumph. They discovered that God's love remained even though they had sinned, and even though they no longer performed the proper rituals for formal worship in the temple.

I first came to that realization later in the same novitiate year which I described earlier. It was a moment that truly changed my life. One day while praying in the chapel, I realized that through my careful observance of the rules I was becoming proud of myself and looking down my spiritual nose at the novices who were less perfect than I was. It dawned on me that my obedience to the law was leading me to love myself rather than God. I was trying to prove my religious worth so that God would have to love me, and I was trying to be spiritually superior so that I could know it for sure.

Suddenly the moment came which more than any other in my life explains why I am the person that I am today. Without saying a word, the Lord told me that he loved me just the way I was. He loved me before, with all my petty faults, and he was loving me now, with all my self-conceit and pride. I didn't have to prove myself to him, because nothing I could do was capable of meriting his infinite love. He just loved me as I was, regardless of whether I was good or bad, just or unjust. And it was that love, not my own worthiness, which made me a child of God. And since nothing could ever take away his love, nothing could ever take away my sonship. I was loved, and that was all that mattered.

That day God's love for me was something that I realized not just in my head but in my heart and in my guts. It was a realization of something so real that I had to bow before it, I had to acknowledge the mystery which suddenly surrounded me. It was not just the thought of God's love for me but the realization of God loving me right there and then which made the difference. It's a realization that I've sometimes lost sight of in my busyness with other things, but it's something that you never forget once it has happened to you. It's the experience of sonship, feeling like a child blessed by the love of a Father who can never love you more and who will never love you less, no matter what you do.

From that moment on, I could see *everything* as grace. I could be thankful for all that God had given me. I could go on my way rejoicing, knowing that I was going to stumble and fall, but not being bothered by that knowledge the way I was before. I did not have to worry about failing, because being perfect didn't matter any more. All that mattered was God's love, and next to that, everything else was insignificant, or even bothersome. I felt like Paul in Philippians 3:7-11:

> But because of Christ, I have come to consider
> all these advantages that I had as disadvantages.
> Not only that, but I believe nothing can happen
> that will outweigh the supreme advantage of
> knowing Christ Jesus my Lord. For him I have
> accepted the loss of everything, and I look on
> everything as so much rubbish if only I can have
> Christ and be given a place in him. I am no
> longer trying for perfection by my own efforts,
> the perfection that comes from the Law, but I
> want only the perfection that comes through
> faith in Christ, and is from God and based on
> faith. All I want is to know Christ and the power
> of his resurrection and to share his sufferings by
> reproducing the pattern of his death.
>
> (Philippians 3:7-11 JB)

This is what the prophets in the exile realized. This is what the author of the Book of Job and some of the other wisdom writers realized. This is the beginning of the realization of the good news of the Gospels. And yet there are people today who have never realized it. There are Christians who have never been truly evangelized, who have never really heard that good news. They still think of God as a policeman in the sky who is keeping track of all their good deeds and bad deeds. They believe that religion is a game of do's and don'ts, and that their job as Christians is to obey all the laws and perform the proper rituals. No wonder that religion often seems to many people like so much bad news!

Who then is the God of the prophets and the wisdom writers? He is a God of mercy and compassion, a forgiving and loving God. Yahweh loves Israel even though, like Hosea's wife, she prostitutes herself before other gods. Yahweh has the patience to wait for her return; he will not be unfaithful to Israel, even though she breaks her promises. Yahweh suffers when she suffers. He goes into exile with her, to be there for her to find in her hour of need. And Yahweh promises to take her by the hand and lead her home, when her banishment is ended.

The Old Testament image which best captures this insight into the heart of God is that of the suffering servant. In the book of Isaiah there are only four servant songs, but they sound a note which develops into a melody and later becomes a major theme of the New Testament. The God who has been revealing himself all along is a lover and a servant. It is not only that our purpose is to know, love and serve God, as the old catechism phrased it, but God's desire seems to be to know, love and serve *us*. That is a wisdom which goes deeper than any catechism answer. That is a revelation which is incredible. That is a truth which is so hard to comprehend that it took generation after generation to slowly start to fathom it.

And yet, looking back, we know this wisdom must be true. Why would God create the universe except out of love? He didn't need it! Why would God free the slaves, or promise them a kingdom, or send prophet after prophet into their midst? It could only be out of love, a love that is patient and forbearing and forgiving. It is a love that is completely self-giving and self-sacrificing.

What a dazzling and overpowering revelation that is! Even when we catch only a glimpse of it, in a moment of spiritual insight, we are almost blown away by it. It seems too good to be true. "Mercy, within mercy, within mercy," as Thomas Merton says.

And so it is. It is indeed too good, from a human point

of view. This is why it took the human race hundreds and even thousands of years to even begin to comprehend it. And this is why, when the prophets first began to perceive this truth, they could not even begin to grasp the enormity of it. In order to perceive it all, they had to see it somehow outside space and time. For God to be God, he had to be completely different from human beings, wholly other, absolutely transcendent. As the Book of Job insists, God is so totally unlike and beyond us, that we can only tremble in awe and marvel at this magnificence. And as the psalmist declares, God's ways are not our ways.

Yet for all its penetration into the depths of God's love, even the prophets' insight was incomplete. They still pictured God "out there," beyond the realm of the human, living at a distance, as it were. When they envisioned his salvation, they portrayed a messiah coming from afar, overturning the wickedness of the world and setting things straight.

And we too, even if we have prophetic faith, can sometimes suffer from this same shortsightedness. We can wonder why God isn't doing more to make people do the right thing. We can refuse to see that God is giving us his power to redeem the world. We can fail to realize that we are the beautiful children of a beautiful and loving God. Yes, it is God's love and his power by which we and all the human race can be redeemed. But as long as we still see this as something that God will do without our participation in his suffering, we do not yet have New Testament faith.

Then again, we can fall into exactly the opposite trap. We can believe that God is so far removed from us that we, by our own efforts, must achieve the salvation which he has promised. We can think that God is calling us to imitate his love, to love others unconditionally, to suffer injustice, to be martyred for this cause or that, to be messiahs saving others from their sins. This sort of approach can even be successful in the short run, for people have done many good things by their own efforts. But ultimately this approach runs out of power, for human willfulness is limited. Ultimately it runs out of love, for human patience wears thin. Ultimately it runs out of vision, for human insight is always shortsighted. And ultimately it runs out of faith, for human conviction is never free from self-doubt.

And so, even beyond the faith of the prophets, even beyond the faith that God is good and loves us unconditionally, there must be yet a deeper faith. It is the faith which the Scriptures do not speak clearly of until the fuller revelation of the New Testament.

Incarnational Faith

In the Gospels and the Book of Acts and throughout the Epistles, a whole new dimension of faith becomes available to those who will accept it. (We shall see this more fully when we take up the New Testament in volume two.) It is a level of living in the Lord which some of the prophesies of Jeremiah and Ezekiel foreshadow, and which is spoken of most clearly by the prophet Joel:

> In the days that follow, I will pour out my spirit
> on everyone. Your sons and daughters shall
> prophesy. Your old men shall dream dreams
> and your young men shall see visions. In those
> days I will pour out my spirit even on your
> servants and your handmaids. (Joel 3:1-2)

Certainly we see the Spirit descending upon Jesus after his baptism in the Jordan, and we see the Spirit again filling the apostles with power on the day of Pentecost. But the very first person to incarnate this new faith was that young girl who said, "Behold the handmaid of the Lord." It was Mary who responded to the angel's announcement that she was to give birth to the messiah with an unconditional yes: "Be it done unto me according to your word" (Luke 1:38).

The final level of faith to which God calls is *a total and unreserved yes to his request to be present in and to the world through us*. He desires to love others unconditionally in and through us. He wants the full redemption of humanity to occur in each of us so that the salvation of the world can be brought about through us.

Those who live at this level of faith can truly be called

125

God's instruments. God wants Light to shine through us, and so our first response to this call is simply to heed it and remain open to his grace. We have to be transparent to God so that he might shine through us. We have to leave the channel open so that the Light might come into the world through us.

Mary is the first person in the Scriptures who understood this completely. She said her yes to God, and her glory is that through her total openness God was able to become incarnate in her. She gave birth to Christ by being so totally open to God's spirit that the child who was born of her was perfectly the Son of God. God loved the world through Jesus; God spoke his message of salvation through Jesus' words; and God's power was manifested through Jesus' deeds.

When the Word became incarnate through Mary's total openness, God formed a body capable of resurrection and eternal life. Jesus was so intimate with the Father who was the source of his being that he called him *Abba*, an expression of great familiarity like "Papa" or "Daddy" in our language. And he himself was so open to the Father's leading that he could follow it even to inevitable conflict, suffering and death, confident that God would not abandon him.

But the incarnation of God in the world did not end with the death of Jesus and his resurrection. God went even further, creating a new body animated by his spirit, worthy of resurrection and filled with eternal life. Its creation began on the day of Pentecost and it grew through people entering into it through Baptism. Its inner life was that of the Holy Spirit and its outer work was the continuation of the work of Jesus. It was that body of Christ which we call the Church.

The Church's call, indeed the call of every Christian, is to be the living body of Christ in history. The Church's function is to be the eyes and ears, mouth and hands of God in the world, a body through which the power of divine love can transform the world. This call is a summons to live at the deepest level of faith, that faith which incarnates God's presence and action in human history. It is a vocation to be in love with ourselves and with every person that we meet, being transformed and transforming every situation with the divine life which flows through us.

When we look at the Church around us, however, we do not see a social body which is full of lovers. We do not see a large group of people who are filled with God's love and who love the world to the point of dedicating themselves to its redemption. We do not see many who totally trust in God, who give without expecting anything in return, who are vulnerable and ready to lay down their lives for others the way the suffering servant did.

The Church's vocation is a call to total surrender: surrender to God, others and the world. But Christians are not called to do this alone and individually but together in the Lord, in the body of Christ. Where love is given and received, where life is shared, where wounds are healed and weakness is strengthened, God's ability to love through us and act through us is amplified. God is able to work through the Church in a powerful way because his love is multiplied in a community of self-sacrificing persons.

And yet we know, when we do experience this sort of Church life, that it is not our own doing. When we pray together, God's spirit prays through us and leads us to intimacy with the Father. When we act as a body, God's power acts through us and effects what we could never do ourselves. God loves through us; he hopes through us; he even has faith through us. This is just another way of saying that God gives us Life in the gifts of faith, hope and love. And so it is all gift; it is all grace. By opening ourselves to these gifts, we become channels of God's grace.

Even if, unfortunately, we do not find many Churches that are living their Christian vocation this fully, and even if we do not see many individuals who are responding eagerly and fully to God's call, we know that such a life is possible from the communities that have existed and do exist in the world, and from the saints both past and present. Two saints who can exemplify this fourth stage of faith for us are St. Francis of Assisi and St. Therese of Lisieux.

St. Francis was impetuously generous even from his youth. As a young man he heard God's call to self-sacrifice, and he responded first by flinging himself into a soldier's life. But when instead of finding glory he was captured and thrown into prison, he listened more closely to discern what God wanted of him. He heard God calling him to rebuild the Church, and without a moment's hesitation he started repairing the ruined chapel in which he liked to pray. Later, when he meditated on the gospel call to poverty, he renounced his father's wealth and cheerfully took up begging, fully trusting that God would take care of all his needs.

Eventually, Francis' humble life of total faith in God attracted a growing group of men and women who shared the life of God which Francis had begun to live. Through their giving of themselves to this common life of faith, the whole medieval Church began to be renewed and rebuilt. St. Francis wanted only to be an instrument of God, and through his willingness to be that instrument, God was able to accomplish more than Francis ever envisioned himself doing.

St. Therese provides a beautiful image of this type of faith. She said she always saw herself in her relationship to God as a little girl. When she first heard the Lord's call she felt like a child standing at the foot of a great staircase, and she saw the Father with loving arms outstretched beckoning her from the top. "Come, Therese, come," he called. Desiring to please him she lifted one little foot and then another, keeping her eyes fixed on his smile. Then, as she neared the top, he bent down and picked her up. In a sweeping movement of grace, God took her to himself. But when, from the safety of his arms she looked back and saw the distance she had come, she realized that it was God who had given her the power to climb the stairs. The Father's love had inspired her and given her direction, and although she had to do her part by responding with her yes at every step, God had from beginning to end been doing it all along. She had not been saving herself, but she had been allowing God to save her.

Our own acts of faith ought to be like those of Francis and Therese. Through prayer we become attuned to God's voice calling us to do his will, calling us to be united with him. Through our decisions and our actions we seek out his direction for us and, no matter what we do, we know that we are going in the right direction if it is leading us toward greater love and greater giving and greater freedom. We do not have to worry about making mistakes, for God will correct us if we are always listening. We do not have to worry about stumbling or falling, for he will be there immediately to catch us.

Life at this level of faith becomes incredibly simple, almost naive. We realize that God does not demand great things of us; he wants only to be great in us. If we allow it, God will even do great things through us. But we ourselves do not have to *make* them happen. We only have to surrender and trust at every step. We only have to hope in him every moment. We only have to stand on his promise and wait for it to be fulfilled in our lives, choosing in accordance with that promise.

As we saw at the beginning of this section, the woman who first completely understood this and totally accepted the Word of God within her was Mary. Through her yes, God took on flesh and became incarnate in a unique way. She lived the life of faith to the fullest. She carried the meaning of faith beyond what it had been for Abraham, the Israelites and the prophets to what it would be for Christians.

Mary lived at the point where the Old and New Testaments meet, and she helped make the transition from the one to the other. As the mother of Christ, she exemplifies what all Christian spirituality would henceforward be. But as a Jewish maiden she also typifies what the spirituality of Israel was always meant to be. The Magnificat, Mary's prayer of praise to God for all that he has done in and through her, provides a New Testament summary of the full meaning of Old Testament faith:

My soul proclaims the greatness of the Lord
and my spirit exults in God my saviour;
because he has looked upon his lowly handmaid.
Yes, from this day forward all generations will
    call me blessed,
for the Almighty has done great things for me.
Holy is his name,
and his mercy reaches from age to age for those
    who fear him.
He has shown the power of his arm,
he has routed the proud of heart.
He has pulled down princes from their thrones

and exalted the lowly.
The hungry he has filled with good things,
the rich sent empty away.
He has come to the help of Israel his servant,
mindful of his mercy
—according to the promise he made to our
ancestors—
of his mercy to Abraham and to his descendants
forever. (Luke 1:46-55 JB)

As a person of faith, Mary is turned completely toward the Lord. She knows in her heart that God is her savior; she has no illusions about saving herself. She praises the Lord and thanks him because she knows that he is doing it all.

At the same time, Mary is aware of a new greatness within herself. She has a sense of her own incredible dignity because the Lord is within her. In our own faith, we come to realize that the Lord is within us and working through us, and this makes us unbelievably great. Not that we are doing anything great, but we are allowing God to do great things in our lives.

If we respect and live in "awe" before the God who is with us (the true meaning of "fear of the Lord"), we allow Power to act through us. When we do that, we see the proud and the mighty cut down to size, and we witness the raising up of the humble and the weak. The poor get fed, the rich get nothing. It's just the opposite of what usually happens in the world, because the world protects its own strength and reverences its own wealth. Those who are already full of themselves cannot receive what God has to give; only those who are empty can be filled.

And so here at the close of the Old Testament and at the threshold of the New Testament, God's promise to Abraham is seeing its fulfillment. At last human faith has evolved to the point where God's action in human history can begin to be recognized for what it is: the activity of God's spirit transforming and redeeming the world through the actions of those who surrender to God's Reign in their lives. At last God's faithfulness comes fully into human history through the faithfulness of those who trust and forgive. At last God's mercy can be shown to all who need it through the mercy of those who are willing to be his servants.

The end of the Old Testament is therefore not the end of the Scriptures. It is not the end of the story of God's faithfulness and mercy, but it is the end of the beginning of the story. The Old Testament brings us to the point where the story of Jesus can begin.

The Great Themes of Scripture: New Testament will take up this story of Jesus and the rest of the story as well—that is, the story of his Spirit and of his Church.